The Chesapeake Collection

*A Treasury of Recipes and
Memorabilia from Maryland's
Eastern Shore*

Tidewater Publishers
Centreville, Maryland

ISBN 0-87033-431-X
Library of Congress Catalog Card No.: 83-50846

Cover illustration by Howard M. Burns

Manufactured in the United States of America
First Tidewater Publishers printing, 1991;
second printing, 1994

The Chesapeake Collection
Cookbook Committee

Beth Adams

Elizabeth Brown

Madaline Brown

Virginia Brown

Elizabeth Callahan

Elizabeth Ecker

Sonya Felipe

Ruth Jones

Sara Kidd

Margaret Myers

Mary Jo Shaffer

Martha Shipe

Jane States

Carol Stockley

Our thanks to Peggy Blades for the illustrations and to the County Commissioners of Caroline County, who generously permitted us to use old photographs from the Caroline County Visual History Collection.

We are indebted to many persons in public life and the innkeepers who allowed us to use their recipes.

Our thanks also go to club members and friends who submitted recipes and served as proofreaders.

TABLE OF CONTENTS

HISTORY OF THE WOMAN'S CLUB OF DENTON, INC.

The Woman's Club of Denton, Inc., founded in 1919 as the Community Club, has a distinguished history of service to the community. Actually, the club was begun in 1915 as a literary society and the members later operated the first public library in rural Caroline County, Maryland.

Beginning as a small group of women in a small town, in 1919 the group joined the County Federation of Woman's Clubs, in 1925 the Maryland Federation, and in 1931 the club joined the General Federation.

The health, education and welfare of the community has always been of prime concern to members of the Woman's Club. Civic projects have included: helping the local volunteer fire company to get its start in 1924; making and serving soup and furnishing clothing to the needy during an extended period of drought in the late 1920's; helping secure the first full-time public health nurse and later a doctor for the county; supplying eyeglasses, milk, and clothing for needy children; sponsoring the first Caroline County Youth Commission; and more.

The club's current largest community service project is the preservation of its clubhouse, a former school house built in 1883. The building is an excellent example of Gothic architecture and was placed on the National Register of Historic Places in 1978.

The sixty members of the club have worked for years holding bake sales, luncheons, house tours, and other fund raisers to maintain the aging building. "The Chesapeake Collection" cookbook is the largest single and the most long-range project that will be used to keep the historic building in the best condition possible.

EASTERN SHORE FLAVOR

Eastern Shore Flavor is disturbingly different because it evokes a feeling of sadness in the hearts of the newcomers for not having discovered it sooner. Even those Marylanders who have not visited the Eastern Shore are shocked to discover culinary sensations that bring on shouts of "Encore." Each new season brings anticipated delicacies that make the Eastern Shore of Maryland truly "God's Country," as the area was affectionately called even in colonial times.

Just where is the Eastern Shore of Maryland? The nine counties of Maryland that border on the eastern fringes of the Chesapeake Bay comprise the Eastern Shore. These counties, from south to north, are Somerset, Worcester, Wicomico, Dorchester, Caroline, Talbot, Queen Annes, Kent, and Cecil. Each of these counties is highly individualistic because each is separated by some of the most beautiful rivers in the world: the Pocomoke River, a haven for oysters, fish, and crabs; the Wicomico River, the setting for Salisbury, the largest city on the Eastern Shore; the Nanticoke River, the meeting ground for Captain John Smith's not too friendly encounter with the mighty tribe of Indians noted for their skills in sorcery; the Choptank River, the location of two county seats, Cambridge and Denton; the Wye River, the scene of British plundering and pillaging during the Revolutionary War; the Chester River, the home of some of the finest moments of trout fishing; the Sassafras River, a picturesque vista of high banks and rolling farmlands; the Elk River, the site of the county seat of Elkton; the Susquehanna River, majestic carver and etcher of the Chesapeake Bay itself; and a host of smaller, but equally distinctive rivers, the Honga, the Little Choptank, the Tred Avon, the Miles, the Corsica, the Bohemia, and the Northeast rivers. Is there any wonder why this area is also called "Tidewater Maryland"?

Eastern Shore Flavor may really come from the tidewater itself, for it is a land of "wetlands." Thousands and thousands of acres of marshes, low-lying scrub pine, myrtle, and cattails are daily covered with the rising and falling tides. It is the habitat of magnificent flocks of migrating wildfowl, deer, rabbit, muskrat (marsh rabbit), fish, oysters, and crabs. In just thinking of Eastern Shore cooking, one thinks of roasted black duck fringed with halved potatoes and several whole onions served with Maryland beaten biscuits and blackberry jelly made during the summer. Although to many Eastern Shoremen it is a crime to serve oysters in any way other than raw on the half shell, scalloped oysters are the "national dish" of the area. The lowly muskrat, when "potted-down" and basted in its own juices, could challenge the highly-touted ambrosia and nectar of the gods. Eastern Shoremen can hardly wait for the warm spring days to "pick a mess of 'spargus' " or for enough warm nights in June to pick their first home-grown tomatoes. The tides that have swept over the land and the salt-spray from nearby rivers and creeks have imbued a flavor that is long to be remembered.

It is not an easy task to characterize Eastern Shore Flavor with words. The subtleties that are its hallmark seem to escape the writer's ability to describe. Eastern Shore Flavor has to be tasted and shared to capture the essence of it. Since most of the early settlements were isolated, families who lived along the thousands of miles of waterfront welcomed the occasional visitor with a warmth that has earned Eastern Shoremen the proud connotation of being the most hospitable people on earth (that is if they like you). Their cooking has the remarkable quality of love. Eastern Shore people would never dare crush their crab meat as is so often found in commercial crab cakes. Instead, crab meat is fondled, lifted, and folded to retain the cherished sweetness. Soft crabs would never be served to the family unless they were moving when they were cleaned. Muskrats would never be cooked until every small piece of fat was removed from the meat. And cooking is never hurried. It is always a source of amazement that the truly great Eastern Shore cook makes all things come out at the peak of perfection at precisely the same time.

Eastern Shore "old timers" would say that Eastern Shore Flavor is not that difficult to describe. Many of them would say "It's the wild taste." Wild geese, ducks, turkeys, rabbits, squirrel, "possum," "coon" and even bear have been an important part of the Eastern Shoreman's life. Good cooks learned to cook a whole potato or onion with wildfowl to remove some of the wildness just as they learned to soak their fish over night to remove the saltiness. The same flavor of wildness went into the dandelion wine, the peach brandy or the "apple jack" that was made at Christmas. Although the old wild flavors have disappeared from the Eastern Shore countryside, there are many who remember and who still strive to keep them in their cooking.

For many who live on the "Shore" the characteristic that best describes Eastern Shore Flavor is seafood—succulent "jimmy" crabs, steamed until they turn bright orange; scalded oysters, dipped in lemon butter; baked rock, stuffed with crab meat; steamed soft shell clams, dipped in their own juices; crispy soft crabs made into a sandwich; or fried clam strips, dipped in horseradish sauce. Even those who cherish their seafood are quick to say, "Don't forget our Delmarvalous chicken." The Shore is noted for both the quality of its chicken and for the secrets of cooking good chicken—chicken touched with orange, chicken wrapped with bacon, chicken marinated in wine, chicken mixed with crab. Yes, it is possible to say Eastern Shore Flavor is a sweet blending of chicken'n seafood.

Eastern Shore Flavor might best be characterized by the simple truth, "a pinch of this and a pinch of that." The really great cooks of the Eastern Shore, when confronted to share their recipes, usually hedge with "Well, I put in a little 'smidgen' of honey, a little 'tad' of onion, a small sliver of fat back ('a strik of lean and a strik of fat'), a handful of walnuts, but then again, I use a handful of raisins if I don't have the nuts."

Eastern Shore Flavor, whether it be a little bit of sorcery from the Nanticokes, a little sign of the sot-weed factor, a remembrance of the call of the wild, a hint of saltiness from the encroaching tides, or a bit of warmth from a strongly independent people, is indeed very different and provocative.

Dr. Thomas A. Flowers
16 Bellevue Avenue
Cambridge, Maryland 21613

The Avalon was just one of the steamboats that cruised the Choptank River well into our century. The boats made several stops at Caroline County wharves. They carried Caroline fruits and vegetables to market in Baltimore, and also transported Caroline Countians to visit the city.

APPETIZERS

BACON YUM-YUMS

2 pounds thick sliced bacon   1½ tablespoons dry mustard
1½ cups brown sugar

Lay bacon in single layer in foil-lined baking pan. Combine brown sugar, and mustard. Sprinkle over bacon. Bake for one hour at 250 degrees. Cut into bite-size pieces. Dry on paper towel.

Yield: 60 pieces
Virginia Brown

CURRY DIP
(for vegetable relish tray)

1 cup mayonnaise   1 teaspoon white vinegar
1 teaspoon curry powder (to your   1 teaspoon onion flakes
   taste)   1 teaspoon garlic salt
1 teaspoon horseradish

Blend well 24 hours before using.

Note: Excellent with relishes or vegetables.

Yield: 1 cup dip
Kay Everngam

CHEESE LAYERS

1 jar Old English cheese   18 thin slices of bread
1 stick butter

Mix butter and cheese. Spread on each slice of bread. Stack in three layers, then cut into bite-size squares. Toast slowly in oven, until cheese melts.

Yield: 96 squares
Virginia Brown

HERBED TOASTS

¼ pound butter
1 teaspoon finely chopped
   parsley, chives and thyme

16 slices of Melba—thin bread

Soften butter. Blend into it 1 well-rounded teaspoon finely chopped parsley, chives and thyme. Spread on Melba-thin slices of bread. Toast in very slow, 200 to 225 degree, oven until dry, not brown. Cut into 1½-inch squares before baking (crust optional).

Yield: 96 pieces
Virginia Brown

OLIVES IN CHEESE BLANKETS

8 ounces sharp cheese, shredded
3 tablespoons margarine
½ cup flour

¼ teaspoon salt
1 5-ounce jar olives

Blend cheese and margarine. Stir in salt and flour. Mold around olives. Place on greased cookie sheet and bake at 400 degrees for 10 to 15 minutes. Freeze before baking, if you don't plan to use them immediately.

Yield: 35 to 40
Virginia Brown

PARTY SANDWICH FILLING

1 8-ounce package cream cheese
   softened
¾ cup chopped walnuts
¼ cup chopped green pepper
3 tablespoons chopped pimiento

1 teaspoon grated onion
1 tablespoon catsup
3 hard cooked eggs, chopped
¾ teaspoon salt
Dash of pepper

Combine all ingredients. Use between buttered slices of sandwich bread.

Yield: 2½ cups
Regina Mueller

MOLDED CHICKEN LIVER PATÉ

¼ teaspoon plain gelatin
¼ cup each water and condensed
   consommé
¾ pound chicken livers
¾ cup soft butter or margarine
3 tablespoons chopped onion
¼ teaspoon salt

¼ teaspoon nutmeg
¼ teaspoon anchovy paste
Dash cayenne
Dash cloves
1 teaspoon dry mustard
Lemon slices and watercress for
   garnish

Soften gelatin in ¼ cup water. Add consommé and heat until dissolved. Pour into 2½ to 3 cup mold. Chill until firm. Cock livers in water and simmer for 20 minutes. Cool, drain, and blend with butter until very smooth. Blend in onions and seasonings. Spread over gelatin and press firmly. Chill. Unmold and garnish with lemon and watercress. Serve with crackers or toast.

Yield: 2 cups
Christine Michael

SHERRIED CHICKEN LIVER PATÉ

1 pound chicken livers
2 tablespoons butter
½ cup chopped onion
4 tablespoons dry sherry
6 tablespoons softened butter

2 tablespoons cognac (brandy)
Pinch thyme
Pinch rosemary
Seasoned salt to taste

Sprinkle livers with small amount of flour to which salt and pepper have been added. Sauté in butter for 5 minutes. Add onion and cook about 3 minutes. Add 2 tablespoons sherry and herbs. Simmer for 1 minute. Add softened butter; purée in electric blender. When blended, add brandy and 2 tablespoons sherry. Add salt and pepper to taste. Chill. Serve with crackers.

Yield: 10 servings
Kay Everngam

PARTY SANDWICH LOAF

1 2-pound loaf unsliced bread
(one day old)
Softened margarine (1 stick)
1 medium can deviled ham
1 jar cheese and pimento spread
4 hard cooked eggs (chopped)
1 6½-ounce can tuna

¾ cup celery (chopped)
¾ cup mayonnaise
2 8-ounce packages cream cheese
4 tablespoons milk
Parsley, radishes, watercress,
carrot curls, for garnish

Slice all crusts from bread. Slice loaf lengthwise into 5 slices. Spread both sides of slices with softened margarine. Prepare tuna salad, ham salad, egg salad, using mayonnaise, celery. Spread slices with salad mixtures and cheese spread. Soften cream cheese with 2 tablespoons milk per package and spread on long sides of loaf first. Spread top last. Garnish with bed of watercress, radishes, and carrot curls. Put parsley around sides.

Note: Chicken salad, shrimp salad, crab salad, also good.

Yield: 15 to 20 servings
Rita Rogers Kearney

SALMON CHEESE BALL

1 16-ounce can red salmon
1 8-ounce package cream cheese
2 tablespoons lemon juice
2 teaspoons horseradish
1 teaspoon Worcestershire sauce
3 teaspoons grated onion

½ teaspoon salt
½ teaspoon liquid smoke
Pinch cayenne
½ cup chopped pecans
3 tablespoons minced parsley

Blend all ingredients except pecans and parsley. Form ball; roll in crushed pecans, and parsley, and chill.

Yield: 1 large or 2 small balls
Kay Everngam

PEPPY CLAM SHELLS

½ cup finely chopped onion
½ cup finely chopped celery
¼ cup finely chopped green
   pepper
4 tablespoons butter
2 tablespoons flour
1 tablespoon Parmesan cheese

¼ teaspoon salt
Dash pepper
Dash hot pepper sauce
½ cup crushed, rich, round
   crackers
1 7½-ounce can minced clams
1 tablespoon butter, melted

In medium skillet cook onion, celery and green pepper in the 4 tablespoons of butter until tender. Stir in flour, cheese and seasonings. Add ½ cup cracker crumbs. Mix well. Stir in undrained clams. Cook and stir until mixture thickens and bubbles. Divide evenly into 4 large baking shells or twelve individual baking shells. Combine remaining crumbs and butter. Sprinkle on top of mixture in each shell. Bake 15 minutes at 350 degrees or until heated through. May be served in small clam shells.

Yield: 12-16 servings
Nellie Dean

ZUCCHINI APPETIZERS

3 cups (4 small) thinly sliced,
   unpared zucchini
1 cup biscuit mix
½ cup chopped onion
½ cup Parmesan cheese
2 tablespoons chopped parsley
½ teaspoon salt

½ teaspoon oregano
½ teaspoon seasoned salt
Dash pepper
1 clove garlic
4 beaten eggs
½ cup vegetable oil

Mix all ingredients. Spread in greased 13x9x2-inch pan. Bake for 25 minutes at 375 degrees. Cut in tiny squares for appetizers or larger squares as accompaniment for main meat dish.

Yield: 16 large squares or 96 small squares
Woman's Club of Denton

15

DILL DIP

½ cup sour cream
⅔ cup mayonnaise
1 tablespoon chopped green onion
   or chives
1 tablespoon chopped fresh
   parsley

1 tablespoon seasoned salt
2 tablespoons fresh dill weed,
   finely chopped
1 teaspoon Worcestershire sauce
Drop or two of hot pepper sauce

Mix and chill. Will keep 4 or 5 days in refrigerator.

Note: May be thinned with vinegar for a salad dressing. I use this with crisp fresh vegetables.

Yield: 1¼ cups
Virginia Warren

HERB CURRY DIP

1 cup mayonnaise or salad
   dressing
½ cup dairy sour cream
1 teaspoon crushed herb mix
¼ teaspoon salt (optional)
⅛ teaspoon curry powder

1 tablespoon snipped parsley
1 tablespoon grated onion
1½ teaspoons lemon juice
½ teaspoon Worcestershire sauce
2 teaspoons capers, drained

Blend all ingredients and chill well. Serve with carrot sticks, celery sticks, broccoli buds, cauliflower buds.

Yield: 8 to 10 servings
Betty J. Brown

HOT OYSTER APPETIZERS

1 pint small oysters
3 tablespoons butter
2 tablespoons lemon juice
2 tablespoons dry white wine

2 teaspoons Worcestershire sauce
3 drops Tabasco
1/8 teaspoon white pepper

In chafing dish melt butter. Add oysters and their liquor, and heat until edges curl. Add lemon juice, wine, and seasonings, and mix gently. Serve hot, on picks, or fondue forks, with crackers or sea toast.

Yield: about 25 single appetizers
Sara Kidd

FRESH FRUIT DIP

1 (8-ounce) package cream cheese
1 (8-ounce) carton sour cream
1 (3½-ounce) can moist coconut
1 (2-ounce) jar crystalized ginger,
    cut up

2 tablespoons confectioners sugar
Pinch of salt

Combine softened cream cheese and sour cream in blender till smooth. Add coconut, ginger, sugar and salt. Mix until blended and dipping consistency (will not be smooth). Refrigerate in covered container. Allow to return to room temperature before serving.

Yield: 2½ cups
Maria Felipe

The Federalsburg Fire Company Band was an integral part of life in that southern Caroline County community in the 1920's. Most small towns had their own community bands in those days.

BEVERAGES

BARBARA JOHNSON'S PUNCH

20 to 25 lemons squeezed
1 small can pineapple juice
1 quart gingerale or club soda

1 pound sugar
Water and orange juice to make
  up the gallon measure

To 1 gallon basic mixture, add 1 fifth rum or whiskey. For party lasting 1 to 2 hours, use 3-5 rounds.

Yield: 33 servings
Beth Adams

FROZEN BRANDY

1 cup water
1 cup sugar
2 tea bags
1 small can frozen orange juice

⅓ to ½ small can lemonade
3½ cups water
½ to ¾ cup bourbon or apricot
  brandy

Boil together the water, sugar and tea bags. Place in large container. Add lemonade, frozen orange juice, water, bourbon or brandy. Freeze. May be refrozen. To serve, thaw to slush stage and serve in punch cups or small glasses.

Yield: 12 punch cups
Mary Jo Shaffer

HOT MULLED CIDER—WASSAIL

1 gallon apple cider
1 quart cranberry juice
3 sticks cinnamon

1 tablespoon allspice
1 tablespoon whole cloves
½ lemon

To the cider add the cranberry juice in a large kettle. In cheesecloth bag put cinnamon, allspice, cloves, and lemon. Simmer slowly for 1 hour or longer. Remove bag of spices and serve hot.

Yield: 30 punch cups
Virginia Brown

FRUIT PUNCH

1 ounce tea
2 pounds sugar
12 lemons
3 quarts sparkling water
6 oranges
1 quart pineapple juice

1 teaspoon almond extract
1 medium size bottle maraschino
   cherries (use strawberries
   in season)
1 teaspoon vanilla

Put tea in pitcher, add 1 quart boiling water, cover and let stand for 20 minutes, then strain. Grate rind from ½ the lemons and oranges. Add grating to sugar and mix with tea. Stir and put on stove and bring to boiling point, and let boil for 5 minutes. Strain into glass jar, let stand over night. Next morning add juice from lemons and oranges. Add other ingredients. When ready to serve, turn into punch bowl on block of ice and add sparkling water. Do not substitute ginger ale for sparkling water as it is too sweet. For the oranges and lemons that you do not have to grate, you may use frozen juice.

Yield: 1½ gallons
Margaret Major Chambers

GAELIC COFFEE

6 or 8 ounce stemmed glass
Hot, black, strong coffee
1 teaspoon sugar

lightly whipped cream
1 jigger Irish whiskey

Gaelic coffee, which is really Irish coffee with an old-fashioned twist, is Mary Canon's "secret recipe". The amount of Irish whiskey suggested is one jigger. The glass should then be filled with hot, black, strong coffee. "The strength of the coffee is the key", insists Ms. Canon. After adding sugar to taste, stir well. Top it off by pouring a lightly whipped cream over the back of a spoon. "The coffee should not be stirred as you add the cream" says Ms. Canon, "since the charm of this drink—apart from its enlivening effect—is the sensation of sipping hot coffee through the cold whipped cream."

Yield: 1 serving
Mary Canon, author for
Harlequin Books

HOT CRANBERRY PUNCH

1 pound fresh cranberries
2 quarts water
2 tablespoons grated orange peel
6 cinnamon sticks

12 whole cloves
4 cups orange juice
1 cup lemon juice
1½ cups sugar

Cook cranberries, water, orange peel, cinnamon, and cloves until berries are soft. Strain. Add the juices and sugar. Heat until sugar is dissolved. Serve hot.

Yield: 25 punch cups
Mary Radcliffe

SWEET POTATO PUNCH

2 medium sized sweet potatoes
2 quarts boiling water
¼ teaspoon salt
1½ cups sugar
1¾ cups pineapple juice
1 12-ounce can undiluted frozen
    orange juice
¼ cup lemon juice

½ teaspoon cinnamon
¼ teaspoon nutmeg
¼ teaspoon mace
5 whole cloves or 2 pinches
    ground cloves
Gingerale or carbonated fruit
    drink
Orange, lemon, strawberries

Peel and slice potatoes into boiling water, add salt and cook until very, very soft. Purée in blender. Cook sugar and juices about 10 minutes, add spices, and bring to boil again. Remove whole cloves. Add sweet potato purée, and stir until well mixed, refrigerate. This mixture will be rather thick. To serve, mix concentrate with 2 or 3 parts gingerale or carbonated fruit drink and pour over ice in punch bowl or pitcher. Garnish with thinly sliced orange, lemon, or strawberries. The concentrate may be frozen. After thawing, mix thoroughly before adding gingerale or carbonated fruit drink.

Yield: ½ gallon concentrate or
    about 1½ gallons punch
Maryland Sweet Potato Association
Peyton Zieger, Home Economist

KICKAPOO JOY JUICE

1 gallon water
16-ounce can concentrated frozen
   orange juice
12-ounce can concentrated
   frozen lemonade

12-ounce can concentrated frozen
   lime juice
⅔ cup granulated sugar

Mix together in large container. Add cranapple juice to flavor and color.

Yield: 5 quarts
Clayton C. Brown

TASTY TOMATO JUICE

3 quarts tomato juice
3 tablespoons sugar (to taste)
1 chopped onion

2 stalks celery
Oregano (pinch)
1 tablespoon vinegar

Combine tomato juice, sugar, onion, and celery. Bring to a boil. Add pinch of oregano, cool. Strain and add 1 tablespoon vinegar. Chill.

Yield: 15 servings
Florence F. Nuttle

DANDELION WINE

2 quarts dandelion blossoms,
   without stems
1 gallon water
3 oranges

3 lemons
3 pounds sugar
¼ cake or ¼ package of yeast

Simmer blossoms in water for one hour (do not boil). Cool, strain. Slice oranges and lemons and add to mixture, along with the sugar. Boil gently for 20 minutes. Cool, strain, and add yeast. Place in clean glass jars. Cover tops with cheese-cloth and leave for three or four weeks, or until fermentation has ceased. Then bottle and cap, or seal.

Ellen Lorraine Johnson

YACHT CLUB PUNCH

1 bottle American champagne　　2 bottles sparkling water
1 gallon sauterne　　　　　　　Brandy to taste

Pour over block of ice. Do not stir.

Yield: 60 punch cups
Everett Adams

ELDERBERRY WINE (COLONIAL)

1 quart elderberry juice　　　　3 pounds sugar
2 quarts warm water

Put in a jug, without stopper. As it works keep filling jug from a bottle of the same liquor kept for the purpose. When sufficiently worked, there will be no bubbles. Strain and bottle.

Yield: 3 quarts
Sara Kidd

DANDELION WINE (COLONIAL)

1 gallon dandelion blossoms　　　3 pounds sugar
　　picked when the sun shines　Pulp of oranges and lemon cut
1 gallon boiling water　　　　　　fine
3 oranges　　　　　　　　　　　2 tablespoons yeast
1 lemon

Pour one gallon of boiling water over dandelion blossoms. Let this stand in a cool place for three days. Then put it into a porcelain lined kettle or one of agate ware, and add the fruit rinds. Boil the mixture 15 minutes, then strain through a flannel bag and add the sugar and pulp of the fruit. When lukewarm, add two tablespoons of yeast and allow the mixture to stand one week in a warm place. Then strain again and let stand three weeks. The wine will be ready for bottling. "This combines the flavor of the best wine with the well known medicinal properties of the dandelion".

Yield: 1½ gallons
Sara Kidd

The school bus, or school wagon, as it was called, was far from the familiar yellow vehicle of today. The wagon was a luxury however to the many rural Caroline children whose alternative was to walk the several miles to school.

SOUPS

BLACK BEAN SOUP

1 pound black beans
6 cups water
2 cups chicken broth
1 cup chopped onion
1 large green pepper (chopped)
1 small sweet red pepper
   (chopped)

3 cloves chopped garlic
3 tablespoons olive oil
2 cans #1 tomatoes
¼ cup white vinegar
2 cups chopped ham
2 teaspoons cumin

Cook beans in 6 cups water with the chicken broth for 2 hours. Sauté onion, peppers, and garlic in olive oil. Cool beans and liquid. Puree ½ of mixture. Cook chopped vegetables until soft. Add tomatoes, vinegar, ham, and cumin. When mixture thickens, add bean puree and whole beans.

Yield: 10-12 servings
Beth Adams

WOMAN'S CLUB CLAM CHOWDER

2 quarts rich chicken broth
   (defatted)
4 strips lean bacon
2 cups chopped celery, including
   tops
2 cups chopped raw potatoes
1 cup chopped carrots
1 can cream style corn

1 can crushed tomatoes
¼ teaspoon dried thyme leaves
½ teaspoon lemon pepper
   seasoning
1 teaspoon parsley flakes
1 cup chopped onions
5 (6½-ounce) cans minced clams
Salt and pepper to taste

Heat chicken broth and add raw vegetables except onions and tomatoes. Fry bacon and remove from fat, crumble and reserve.
   Sauté onion in bacon fat and add to broth and vegetables. Simmer until potatoes are tender. Add corn, seasonings, and minced clams. Taste for seasoning and adjust. Simmer until flavors are blended, at least 15 minutes. Add crumbled bacon and serve very hot.

Yield: 4 quarts
Woman's Club

WOMAN'S CLUB CHICKEN AND DUMPLING SOUP

3½ quarts chicken broth
2 teaspoons salt
2 cups finely chopped celery
    leaves
2 cups cooked and cut up
    chicken, or more if desired

¼ recipe of slippery dumplings
    (about 60 dumplings), refer
    to slippery dumpling recipe

Heat chicken broth to boiling. Add celery leaves, salt, and cut up
chicken. Bring back to boil and cook for five minutes. Add dumplings,
cover and cook for about 8 to 10 minutes, until dumplings are done.

Yield: 1 gallon soup
    16 to 20 servings
Woman's Club of Denton, Inc.

SLIPPERY DUMPLINGS
(Old Eastern Shore Recipe)

6 cups flour
½ cup vegetable shortening

6 teaspoons baking powder
1 teaspoon salt

Mix all ingredients and add 2½ to 3 cups *hot* water until dough is easy
to handle. Knead until smooth texture; then roll out thin. Cut into
squares. Drop into boiling chicken broth. Boil until they cut easily with
fork. Can be used for chicken dumplings or chicken dumpling soup.

Yield: 200 2x2 dumplings
Woman's Club of Denton, Inc.

CRAB SOUP, EASTERN SHORE STYLE

2 pounds stew meat, cut in
   1-inch cubes
2 large onions, chopped
4 stalks celery, chopped
1 bunch carrots, cut in cubes
   or slices
2 pounds potatoes, cut in cubes
1 20-ounce package frozen lima
   beans
1 20-ounce package frozen peas
1 20-ounce package frozen corn

1 20-ounce package frozen green
   beans
3 15-ounce cans tomatoes
1 pound bacon, fried until crisp
   and crumbled, save some of
   the grease
2 pounds crab meat
1 bay leaf
3 quarts water, or as much as
   you like
Salt and pepper to taste

Brown stew meat, add 2 quarts water, celery, onions, carrots, bay leaf, simmer one hour. Add potatoes, lima beans, peas, corn, green beans, one quart water, simmer another hour. Add tomatoes, salt and pepper to taste. Take out bay leaf. Add crab meat and bacon, simmer about 30 minues. Add about ½ cup flour to one cup water, stir until dissolved, then add to soup. Stir until thickened. Freezes well.

Yield: About 30 servings.
Mrs. Flo Berton

CRAB SOUP

1 quart water
3 beef bouillon cubes
2 1-pound cans crushed tomatoes
1 tablespoon Old Bay seasoning
1 medium white onion, chopped

2 medium carrots, chopped
½ green bell pepper, chopped
1 stalk celery, chopped
1 1-pound can mixed vegetables
8 ounces back fin crabmeat

Dissolve bouillon cubes in 1 quart hot water. Add crushed tomatoes. Bring to a low boil. Add chopped vegetables, cook until tender. Add mixed vegetables and seasoning. Add crabmeat. Do not boil, as crabmeat will shred.

Yield: 4 to 6 servings
Robin Hickman
Stone Hearth Inn

BAYSIDE INN'S CRAB SOUP

1 pound regular crabmeat
3 16-ounce cans mixed vegetables
1 16-ounce can whole tomatoes
   (mashed)
1 6-ounce can tomato paste
5 cups water

1 medium onion (chopped)
1 stalk celery (chopped)
1 teaspoon Old Bay Seafood
   Seasoning
Salt and pepper to taste

Mix all ingredients except crabmeat. Cook over medium heat one hour. Add 1 pound regular crabmeat. Do not boil as crabmeat will flake easily.

Yield: 16 to 20 servings
Capt. Alan Tyler

CRAB SOUP

2 quarts tomatoes (canned)
1 can tomato juice
1 medium onion
⅔ cup diced celery
3 cups diced potatoes
2 large bags mixed vegetables
   (20 to 24 ounces)

4 to 8 tablespoons Old Bay
   Seasoning
Salt
Sugar
1 pound regular crabmeat

Bring 3 quarts of lightly salted water to a boil, add the 2 quarts of hand crushed and cored tomatoes and tomato juice and bring to a boil again. Add diced onion, celery, and potatoes. Add 2 tablespoons seafood seasoning and 2 tablespoons sugar. Boil on medium heat aproximately 20 to 30 minutes. Then add 2 large bags of mixed vegetables (be sure they include carrots, peas, corn, string beans, and limas). If any of these are not in mixture, add separate regular-size boxes. Taste often and add seafood seasoning until the soup is slightly hot in taste. Also add more salt if needed. Never use cabbage or turnips in crab soup. After adding all vegetables, add 1 pound regular crabmeat and simmer until vegetables are tender but not soft (approximately 45 minutes to 1 hour). This is better the next day and will keep in refrigerator several days. As you cook the soup, add water if necessary, to make about 1½ gallons when finished.

Yield: 1½ gallons
Carolyn Becker

CHICKEN ASPARAGUS SOUP

1 tablespoon oil
1 clove garlic (minced)
1 small onion sliced
2 cups cooked, diced chicken
4 cups chicken stock
1 teaspoon salt
Dash pepper

1 tablespoon minute tapioca or
2 tablespoon cornstarch dissolved
   in ¼ cup water
1 can (12-ounce) asparagus tips
   and stems
⅓ cup diced cooked ham
1 egg white beaten till stiff

In medium sauce pan heat oil, add garlic and onion. Sauté until onion is transparent. Add chicken, sauté 3 minutes.

Add stock or bouillon and liquid from asparagus can. Season with salt and pepper. Bring to boil. Add tapioca or cornstarch, lower heat and simmer 30 minutes (If using cornstarch, add just before stirring in egg white).

Add asparagus and ham. Simmer 5 minutes. Gently stir in egg white. Remove from heat. May sprinkle chopped green onion on top.

Yield: 6-8 servings
Sonya Felipe

CHICKEN CORN SOUP

One 4 to 5 pound stewing chicken
3 quarts cold water
1 tablespoon salt
¼ teaspoon pepper
1 onion
1 stalk celery

3 cups young sweet corn cut
   off cob or canned corn,
   cream style
1½ cups flour
½ teaspoon salt
1 egg, slightly beaten

Boil chicken with salt, pepper, onion, and celery until meat is tender. Remove chicken from bones and reserve some of the best pieces for pot pie or other use. Cut enough of the chicken to make two cups. Strain the broth and add water if necessary to make two quarts. Bring broth to boiling point and put in cut chicken, corn, and rivels, which have been made by rubbing flour, ½ teaspoon salt, and beaten egg together between the palms of the hands to form small lumps. Stir constantly while rivels are being added. Cook about 10 minutes or until rivels are done, stirring occasionally. Serve very hot garnished with chopped parsley if desired. Cooked rivels should have about the texture of boiled rice.

Yield: 8 or 10 servings
Sara Kidd

CAZUELA DE AVE
(chicken soup)

1 chicken cut up
2 pounds potatoes, cut in chunks
1 onion
4 tablespoons oil
1½ cups green beans
1 cup corn
1 cup peas

1 cup rice (raw)
1 cup cut up pumpkin or
   butternut squash
1 tablespoon paprika
1 tablespoon oregano
½ tablespoon cumin
Salt and pepper

Brown chicken in oil, cover with water and simmer for 20 minutes. Add rest of ingredients and cook for 25 minutes more. Serve in soup bowls.

Yield: 10-12 servings
Carmen B. Howell

WOMAN'S CLUB CORN CHOWDER

8 slices bacon (chopped)
2 cups chopped onion
8 cups diced potatoes
3 #2½ cans cream style corn
1 quart whole milk
2 (13-ounce) cans evaporated milk

1 quart water
¾ teaspoon pepper
¼ pound butter (1 stick)
1 tablespoon salt
1 tablespoon sugar
Chopped parsley

Sauté chopped bacon and onion in heavy frying pan. Transfer to large kettle; add potatoes and water and cook until potatoes are tender. Add all other ingredients and simmer until very hot. Serve with chopped parsley on top of each bowl of soup.

Yield: 16 to 20 servings
Woman's Club of Denton Inc.

"Ring around the moon, bad weather follows soon. Rain before seven, clear before eleven".

CREAM SOUPS

¼ cup butter
¼ cup flour
4 cups milk or
    2 cups milk and 2 cups
    chicken or beef broth

⅛ teaspoon pepper
¾ teaspoon salt

Melt butter and blend in flour to make a smooth roux. Add milk or milk and broth gradually, and bring to a boil. Reduce heat and stir until smooth. Add salt and pepper. This is basic white sauce.

This sauce may be used as the base for many cream soups by the addition of chopped cooked vegetables such as broccoli, kale, spinach, asparagus, celery, or mushrooms. Cream of tomato soup may be made by adding 2 cups of hot, cooked, crushed, or puréed tomatoes gradually to 2 cups hot basic white sauce. The addition of ½ teaspoon baking soda to the hot tomatoes will help to prevent curdling. Stir the tomato soup constantly with a wooden spoon and serve at once.

Yield: 4-6 servings
Sara Kidd

CUCUMBER VICHYSOISSE

2 cucumbers peeled, seeded, and
    chopped
1 pound potatoes peeled and
    diced
2 leeks chopped, including green
    tops

4 cups chicken broth
Salt and pepper to taste
2 cups milk
½ cup sour cream
1 teaspoon curry powder

Set aside ½ of cucumbers. Put rest with potatoes, leeks, and broth in pan. Bring to boil, simmer until vegetables are tender. Put mixture thru blender. Add rest of cucumbers and milk. Bring to boil and simmer 10 minutes. Chill. Serve topped with a spoonful of sour cream and dash of curry powder.

Yield: 10 to 12 servings
Beth Adams

S
O
U
P
S

CLAM SOUP

1 can pepperpot soup
1 can cream of celery soup
1 6½-ounce can minced clams
   with juice

1 soup can milk
¼ cup sherry
Dash hot pepper sauce
¼ cup chopped parsley

Mix soup, clams, hot pepper sauce, and milk. Simmer until very hot. Add sherry and serve. Float parsley on top.

Yield: 6 to 8 servings
Dolly Moore

CREAMY CARROT SOUP

2 tablespoons margarine
½ cup chopped onion
Two 13-ounce cans chicken broth
¼ teaspoon salt

One 8-ounce can evaporated milk
2½ cups diced carrots
3 tablespoons flour
⅛ teaspoon nutmeg

Sauté onions and 2 cups carrots; stir in flour; add broth and cook until thickened. Simmer covered for 15 minutes. Add salt, nutmeg, and purée. Add evaporated milk and heat. Sprinkle ½ cup carrots and chopped parsley over soup when serving.

Yield: 6 servings
Beth Adams

CABBAGE SOUP

1 head green cabbage shredded
1 pint leftover beef or pork gravy

Salt and pepper to flavor
2 tablespoons vinegar

Slightly dilute gravy for soup stock. Add shredded cabbage and salt and pepper and vinegar. Cook until soft but not mushy. Should have slight crispness.
   Especially good served with Polish sausage.

Yield: 6 servings
Lois Pelosky

GAZPACHO

2 large tomatoes, peeled
1 large cucumber, peeled
1 medium onion
1 medium green pepper
1 pimento, drained
2 cans (12-ounce) tomato juice
⅓ cup olive oil

⅓ cup wine vinegar
⅛ teaspoon pepper
1½ teaspoons salt
¼ teaspoon hot pepper sauce
2 cloves garlic
½ cup croutons
¼ cup chopped chives

Cut tomatoes, ½ cucumber, ½ onion, ¼ pepper, ¼ pimento in small pieces. Blend with ½ cup tomato juice at high speed. Mix purée with rest of tomato juice, 4 tablespoons olive oil, vinegar, hot sauce, and seasonings. Cover and refrigerate 2 hours. Rub skillet with garlic; reserve garlic. Sauté croutons in rest of olive oil until browned. Chop rest of vegetables, place in separate bowls to serve as garnishes. Add crushed garlic to soup at serving time.

Yield: 6 servings
Beth Adams

TOMATO BEAN SOUP

2 cups navy beans
1 teaspoon soda
1 quart boiling water
¼ teaspoon pepper
1½ teaspoons sugar

1 medium onion chopped
1 quart tomatoes
1 or 2 teaspoons salt
½ pound salt pork cut in ½-inch
    pieces

Soak beans overnight in soda and boiling water. Drain and rinse. Place in kettle with water to cover, and salt pork and onion. Boil; reduce heat and cover. Cook 4 hours, adding more water if necessary. Stir in tomatoes, sugar, salt, and pepper. Heat to boiling, reduce heat. Cook 1 hour. (Better heated up the second day). If you can't get salt pork, ham or bacon will do.

Yield: 10 servings
Vera Van Schaick

WOMAN'S CLUB VEGETABLE-BEEF SOUP

3 quarts water
2 pounds beef bones
1½ pounds boneless chuck beef
2 large cans stewed tomatoes
2 cups turnips, diced
2 cups potatoes, diced
2 cups celery, chopped
1 cup onions, chopped
2 cups cabbage, chopped

10-ounce package frozen mixed
   vegetables
1 tablespoon salt
2 teaspoons pepper corns
1 bay leaf
1 bouquet garni (sprigs of thyme,
   parsley, oregano, etc., as
   desired)

Crack beef bones and cover with 3 quarts water. Add salt, bouquet garni, pepper corns, and bay leaf. Cover and simmer 3 or 4 hours to make 2 quarts beef stock, adding water if necessary.

Chop and brown chuck beef and add to stock. Simmer until beef is tender, adding water as needed.

Add all vegetables and cook until vegetables are tender. Taste and adjust seasonings.

One-fourth recipe of slippery dumplings may be added if desired. Cook dumplings 8 to 10 minutes.

Yield: 16 to 20 servings
Woman's Club of Denton, Inc.

TILGHMAN'S DELIGHT
OYSTER STEW

1 pint oysters—wash
½ stick butter
1 pint milk

½ pint cream (canned will do)
Pinch of salt

Add butter to oysters in saucepan and heat until oysters curl. Add milk, cream and salt, and heat, but do not boil.

Yield: 4 servings
"Butterfly"

Dr. William Wroten, a History professor at Salisbury Teacher's College had this to say about the Eastern Shore: "It's been said that the Lord made the Earth in six days and rested on the seventh. On the eighth day He made the Eastern Shore." How true!

OYSTER STEW

1 pint oysters (or 2 dozen fresh
    shucked)
1 can evaporated milk
1 cup whole milk

3 tablespoons butter
1 teaspoon Worcestershire sauce
Dash of cayenne pepper (optional)
Salt to taste

Heat undrained oysters. Combine with 1 tablespoon butter and other ingredients, except milk, in heavy sauce pan until edges of oysters curl. While oysters are cooking, combine and heat to simmer evaporated and whole milk. When oysters are done, stir in simmering milk. Serve in bowls topped with remaining butter.

Yield: 4 servings
L. T. Short

Mills were numerous in rural areas years ago. Various commodities were produced by water power, including the flour that was ground in this mill from local farmers' wheat.

BREADS

TRADITIONAL
MARYLAND BEATEN BISCUITS

7 cups flour
1 cup lard

1 teaspoon salt

Work together the flour, lard, and salt. Add enough water to make a stiff dough. Beat with an ax (scout ax) on heavy wooden surface. Shape into small biscuits, prick top of biscuits with a fork. Bake 20 minutes in hot oven (425 degrees).

Yield: about 5 to 6 dozen
Mrs. Caroline L. Wheatley

GOLDEN LEMON BUTTER

6 eggs
2 egg yolks
2 cups sugar

Rind and juice of 4 lemons
1 cup butter or margarine

Stir eggs and sugar together in top of double boiler. Add lemon rind and juice and butter. Cook over gently boiling water until smooth and thick as mayonnaise. (Used as a spread for Maryland biscuits "in the olden days").

Yield: 2 pints
Caroline Allaband

BISCUITS SUPREME

2 cups sifted flour
4 teaspoons baking powder
½ teaspoon salt
⅔ cup milk

½ teaspoon cream of tartar
2 teaspoons sugar
½ cup vegetable shortening

Sift together dry ingredients, cut in vegetable shortening until like coarse crumbs. Add milk all at once, stirring just until dough follows fork around bowl. Turn out on floured surface, knead gently ½ minute. Pat ½ inch thick and cut with biscuit cutter. Bake on ungreased pan for 10-12 minutes at 450 degrees.

Yield: 16-18 biscuits
Kay Everngam

ANDREW'S APPLE BREAD

½ cup butter or lard
½ cup sugar
½ cup dark brown sugar
½ cup milk (cold)
1 egg well beaten
2 cups sifted flour

½ teaspoon salt
1 teaspoon baking soda (scant)
1 teaspoon baking powder
½ teaspoon ground cinnamon
1 cup chopped apples (unpeeled, cored)

Cream butter (lard) with sugars. Combine milk with beaten egg and stir well into creamed mixture. Sift flour, salt, baking soda, baking powder and cinnamon together over the chopped apples. Blend well and combine with milk, egg, sugar mixture, stirring enough to dampen flour. Turn dough into well greased loaf pan. Let stand 15 to 20 minutes. Then bake 1 hour at 350 degrees. Delicious warm!

Yield: 1 loaf
Andrew Myers

BISCUITS

3 cups all-purpose flour
2½ tablespoons sugar
4½ teaspoons baking powder
¾ teaspoon salt

¾ teaspoon cream of tartar
¾ cup butter or margarine
¾ cup milk
1 egg, beaten lightly

Sift together into a bowl, flour, sugar, baking powder, salt, and cream of tartar. Add butter or margarine. With a fork or pastry blender, blend mixture until it resembles coarse meal, then stir in egg and milk. Turn dough on a lightly floured surface; knead lightly for 4 or 5 strokes. Roll or pat into a ½ inch thick round. Cut with a 2-inch biscuit cutter. Place on a baking sheet and bake in a preheated 425 degree oven for 10 to 12 minutes.

Yield: 20 to 24 biscuits
Jane (Johnson) States

SWEET POTATO BISCUITS

6 tablespoons shortening
2 medium sized sweet potatoes,
  cooked and mashed
2 cups flour

3 teaspoons baking powder
4 tablespoons sugar
1 teaspoon salt
½ cup milk

Sift together flour, baking powder, and salt. Add sugar and shortening to sweet potatoes while hot. Combine potato and flour mixture with milk. Knead for 1 minute. Roll or pat to ¾-inch thickness. Cut out and bake at 400 degrees for 12 to 15 minutes.

Yield: 2 dozen biscuits
Helen Bozman

SWEET POTATO BISCUITS

2 cups warm mashed sweet
  potatoes
½ cup shortening (butter)
⅔ cup sugar

1 teaspoon salt
3 cups flour
4 teaspoons baking powder

Mix potatoes, shortening, sugar, and salt. Add dry ingredients. Roll out on slightly floured board. Cut out with biscuit cutter. Bake at 425 degrees for 12 to 15 minutes.

Yield: 2 dozen
Caroline M. Allaband

CRANBERRY BREAD

2¼ cups flour
2 teaspoons baking powder
½ teaspoon salt
¾ cup brown sugar
2 tablespoons butter
1 egg

1 cup ground raw cranberries
½ cup orange marmalade
¼ cup boiling water
1 teaspoon baking soda
½ cup chopped pecans
½ cup golden raisins

Mix everything together. Turn into 2 greased 8x4x2-inch loaf pans and bake at 350 degrees for 50 minutes.

Yield: two 8x4x2-inch loaves
Marianne Kent

BANANA-ORANGE BREAD

2 cups flour
½ teaspoon baking powder
½ teaspoon baking soda
¼ teaspoon salt
¼ cup butter
½ cup chopped black walnuts

¾ cup sugar
1 large egg
¾ cup (2 medium) mashed
    bananas
1 tablespoon grated orange rind
3 tablespoons orange juice

Cream butter and sugar. Add egg, beat well. Add mashed bananas, orange rind, and juice. Add sifted dry ingredients and nuts. Mix well, bake in greased loaf pan at 350 degrees for 1 hour.

Yield: 1 loaf
Kay Everngam

SWEET SURPRISES

¾ cup raisins
1 cup boiling water
1 teaspoon baking soda
2 egg yolks in a cup
Mayonnaise
1 teaspoon vanilla
1 cup sugar
2 cups self-rising flour

¼ teaspoon salt
¼ teaspoon mace
1 cup nuts, finely chopped
1 cup shredded raw (peeled) sweet
    potato using medium size
    shredder
1 tablespoon lemon juice

Mix dry ingredients, add nuts and shredded sweet potato that has been sprinkled with lemon juice. Mix raisins, boiling water, and soda, and cool to lukewarm. Add mayonnaise to egg yolks to make ¾ cup. Add vanilla. Stir raisin and egg yolk mixtures into dry ingredient mixture. Mix well. Pour in greased and floured 13x9-inch pans (2) or (3) 8x8-inch pans. Sprinkle top with mixture of cinnamon and sugar. Bake at 350 degrees for 25 minutes. Cut into bars when cold. May also be baked in loaf pans. Freezes well.

Note: Easy to make, moist and delicious, with surprising ingredients. Mayonnaise, and self-rising flour, and shredded raw sweet potatoes. Good for breakfast, as a snack or dessert. After sampling a plate full of these with a glass of milk, a neighbor (an 11 year old boy) took the recipe home and made them himself. So believe me, they are "easy to make"!

Yield: 48 bars
Peyton Zieger

JOHNNY CAKE

METHOD I

1 cup sugar	2 teaspoons soda
1 egg	2 cups sour milk
2 tablespoons shortening	1½ cups flour
Pinch of salt	1 cup corn meal

Cream sugar, egg, shortening, and salt. Dissolve soda in sour milk, and mix well. Add flour and corn meal to creamed mixture. Add milk. Put in 8x8-inch greased pan. Bake one hour in 350 degree oven.

METHOD II

1 cup sugar	2 teaspoons baking powder
1 egg	2 cups milk
2 tablespoons shortening	1 cup flour
Pinch of salt	1 cup corn meal

Cream sugar, egg, shortening, and salt. Add baking powder, flour, and corn meal. Add milk. Put in 8x8-inch greased pan or iron skillet. Bake one hour in 350 degree oven.

Yield: twelve servings
Mrs. Rita Seely

JOHNNY CAKE

1 cup corn meal (yellow)	1 egg
1 cup flour	¼ cup sugar
1 cup milk	4 teaspoons baking powder
¼ cup shortening	

Combine, bake in greased 8-inch square pan at 350 degrees for 20 to 25 minutes.

Yield: 12 to 15 servings
Ruth Evans

JOURNEY CAKES

1 cup stone ground white corn
   meal
1 teaspoon salt

1 teaspoon sugar (optional)
1¼ cups boiling water

Combine meal, salt, and sugar. Stir in water until mixture is smooth. Batter will be thick. Drop by tablespoons on a well greased griddle and fry over moderate heat about 6 minutes. Turn and fry second side. If thinner batter is desired, thin with ½ cup milk or water. A crisper cake will result. Serve with maple syrup. OLD SAYING ABOUT JOURNEY CAKES "thru the mill, ground and bolted and come out a regular-built-down east Journey Cake. When hot, damned good but when cold, damned sour and indigestible. I'm the same way!"

Yield: 8 to 10 servings
Beth Adams

GOLDEN THREAD LOAF

2 cups flour
1 cup sugar
1½ teaspoons baking powder
1¼ teaspoons salt
½ teaspoon soda
¼ teaspoon mace
¼ cup shortening

1 egg
¼ cup frozen orange juice
½ cup water
1½ cups shredded raw sweet
   potatoes
¼ cup (or more) raisins
1 tablespoon lemon juice

Mix dry ingredients, cut in shortening. Beat egg, add orange juice and water, mixed together. Blend into dry ingredients until moistened. Fold in shredded sweet potatoes and raisins that have been sprinkled with lemon juice. Fill greased and floured loaf pans ½ to ⅔ full and sprinkle cinnamon and sugar on top. Bake at 350 degrees for 30 to 40 minutes. Use two regular size loaf pans or four mini size. Freezes well. Can also be baked in square or oblong pans and cut into squares to serve.

Yield: 2 loaves
Peyton Zieger

COWBOY COFFEE CAKE

2½ cups flour
½ teaspoon salt
2 cups brown sugar
⅔ cups vegetable shortening
2 teaspoons baking powder

½ teaspoon soda
½ teaspoon cinnamon
½ teaspoon nutmeg
1 cup sour milk
2 eggs

Combine first 4 ingredients. Reserve ½ cup. To remaining crumbs, add baking powder, soda, and spices. Mix well. Add milk and eggs. Pour into 2 cake pans or square pans. Sprinkle crumbs on top. Chopped nuts and cinnamon may be added to crumbs on top. Bake at 375 degrees for 25 to 30 minutes.

Note: To make sour milk add 1 tablespoon vinegar to 1 cup milk.

Yield: 18 to 24 servings
Kay Everngam

STEAMED BROWN BREAD

1 cup whole wheat flour
1 cup yellow corn meal
1 cup white flour
1 cup molasses

½ cup raisins
1 teaspoon baking soda
1½ cups hot water

Mix the above ingredients together. Grease a pudding mold or 2-pound coffee can and fill ⅔ full. Cover, place on rack in large covered kettle one-half full of hot water and steam 3 hours. Invert on rack to cool. Cover with towel during cooling period. To cut, wrap a length of string around the loaf. Cross the ends, tighten so string slices thru the loaf. This prevents soggy, crumbly slices. May be frozen.

Yield: 1 large loaf
Hannah Adams

To be sure your eggs will hatch, put nails under the pine shatts in the nest.

MOTHER WHITING'S GRAHAM GEMS

1 egg
1 cup milk
2 tablespoons melted butter
2 cups graham flour (whole
    wheat)

2 teaspoons cream of tartar
Dash salt
4 tablespoons sugar
1 teaspoon soda

Beat egg, add milk, butter, sugar, and salt. Add rest of ingredients. Bake in 400 degree oven 20 to 25 minutes. If using a gem pan, they will cook more quickly than a muffin tin.

Yield: 12 muffins
Beth Adams

YELLOW SQUASH MUFFINS

2 pounds yellow squash (about 8
    medium size)
2 eggs
1 cup butter or margarine, melted
1 cup sugar

3 cups all-purpose flour
1 tablespoon plus 2 teaspoons
    baking powder
1 teaspoon salt

Wash squash thoroughly; trim off ends. Cut into 1-inch slices. Cook in small amount of boiling water 15 minutes, or until tender. Drain well; mash. Measure enough to make 2 cups. Combine squash, eggs, and butter; stir well and set aside. Combine remaining ingredients in large bowl. Make a well in center of mixture. Add squash mixture and stir just enough to moisten. Spoon into greased muffin tins, filling ¾ full. Bake for 20 minutes at 350 degrees, or until wooden toothpick inserted in center comes out clean.

Yield: 1½ dozen muffins
Helen Bozman

MONKEY CAKE

24 buttermilk biscuits
1 cup sugar

1½ sticks butter
1 tablespoon cinnamon

Cut biscuits in 4 pieces. Roll into balls in sugar and cinnamon. Drop in tube pan (greased). Take remaining sugar and cinnamon and cook in butter until it comes to a boil. Pour over top of biscuits. Bake at 350 degrees for 45 minutes. Serve hot.

Yield: 15 slices
Kay Howell

NUT BREAD

1 cup sugar
1 cup milk
1 egg
3½ cups flour

2 teaspoons baking powder
½ teaspoon salt
1 cup chopped nuts

Mix in order named. Put in greased loaf pan and let stand 15 minutes before baking. Bake 1 hour in slow oven (300 degrees). May be baked in two small pans.

Yield: 1 loaf
Kay Everngam

BANANA ORANGE LOAF

1¾ cups flour
⅔ cup sugar
1 teaspoon baking powder
½ teaspoon salt
¼ teaspoon baking soda

½ cup shortening
1 cup mashed bananas
2 eggs
1 teaspoon orange extract

Mix first 5 ingredients. Cut in shortening until mixture resembles coarse crumbs. Stir in bananas, eggs, and orange extract just until blended. Bake 1 hour at 350 degrees in 9x5 inch loaf pan.

Yield: one 9x5 loaf
Marianne Kent

HERBED CROUTONS

6 slices firm white bread—crusts
   removed
4 tablespoons salted butter or
   margarine

1 teaspoon dried parsley
1 teaspoon dried tarragon
1 teaspoon dried rosemary

Cut bread into ½-inch squares. In a large heavy frying pan, melt butter over medium heat. Crush the herbs finely between your hands or in a mortar and pestle and stir into hot butter. Sauté bread cubes into butter until lightly browned on all sides. Drain on paper towels and let cool.

Note: Croutons for soup, salads, and casseroles.

Yield: 3 cups
Joyce Zeigler
(From King Clan Cook Book)

DATE AND NUT BREAD

1 cup chopped dates
¾ cup chopped nuts
1½ teaspoons baking soda
2 eggs
3 tablespoons butter

1 cup sugar
1½ cups flour
1 cup boiling water
½ teaspoon vanilla
Pinch of salt

Put nuts, dates, butter, and soda in a bowl and add water. Beat eggs and add sugar to them, blending thoroughly. Combine with flour, then mix the two combinations. Add vanilla. Pour into well greased loaf pan, filling about ⅔ full. Bake 30 minutes to 45 minutes in a moderate oven. Remove from pan while hot.

Yield: 1 loaf
Mrs. Edith Merriken

BANANA PANCAKES

1 egg
2 cups milk
2 tablespoons melted butter

2 cups pancake flour
1 cup banana pulp

Slightly beat egg. Add milk and butter. Mix well. Add liquid to pancake flour and banana pulp. Beat until smooth. Pour small pancakes on hot griddle, turning only once.

Yield: 2 dozen medium pancakes
Ellen Lorraine Johnson

WALTON'S HEALTH BREAD

1 quart bran
1 quart white flour
1 pint sour cream
½ cup molasses

1 teaspoon baking soda
½ cup chopped nuts
½ cup chopped raisins

Dissolve soda in molasses and mix with all other ingredients. Turn into two bread pans and bake for 45 minutes to 1 hour at 350 degrees.

Yield: 2 loaves
Walton Avery Johnson

CORN BREAD

1 cup corn meal
1 cup flour
¼ cup sugar
½ teaspoon salt

4 teaspoons baking powder
1 egg
1 cup milk
¼ cup shortening

Sift together dry ingredients into bowl. Add egg, milk, and shortening. Beat until smooth (about 1 minute). Bake in greased 8-inch square pan or greased muffin pans in hot oven, 425 degrees, 20 to 25 minutes. Serve warm with butter or covered with creamed chicken, fish, or meat.

Yield: 12 squares or 12 2-inch muffins
Mrs. Jeanette Blake

OATMEAL BREAD

1 cup rolled oats
½ cup brown sugar
2 teaspoons salt
5 cups flour

1 tablespoon shortening
2 cups milk (scalded)
2 yeast cakes

Mix oats, sugar, salt, and shortening. Pour over the scalded milk. Let stand until lukewarm. Add yeast. Add about 4 cups flour and beat. Add more flour until mixture no longer clings to bowl or fingers. Cover, let rise until double (about 2 hours). Divide dough with metal spoon dipped in cold water. Place in loaf pans, press top with wet spoon until level. Grease tops of loaves. Let double again, covered. Bake at 450 degrees 10 to 15 minutes. Reduce heat to 350 degrees and let bake 40 to 45 minutes. Turn out on rack to cool.

Yield: 2 loaves
Nancy Adams

HOBO BREAD

1 box raisins
2 cups boiling water
4 teaspoons baking soda
2 cups sugar

1 teaspoon salt
½ cup salad oil
4 cups sifted flour

Soak raisins in boiling water. When lukewarm add baking soda. Cover and let stand overnight. Add sugar, salt, and oil. Add flour, 1 cup at a time, stirring well. This will be very thick. Grease and flour 3 1-pound coffee cans. Fill ½ full and bake at 350 degrees for 1 hour and 10 minutes. Let stand 10 minutes, then shake out of can gently. Can be wrapped, frozen, and kept for months in freezer.

Yield: 3 1-lb. loaves
Mildred James

SWEET POTATO YEAST ROLLS

⅔ cup shortening
⅔ cup sugar
1 cup mashed sweet potatoes
1 yeast cake dissolved in ½
    cup lukewarm water

2 eggs (well beaten)
1 cup scalded milk
1 teaspoon salt
5 cups flour

Mix potatoes, milk, shortening, salt, and sugar. Add yeast, mix well and add eggs. Add flour and knead well. May need just a little more flour. Cover with damp cloth and let rise. Knead again. Make into rolls and bake in 400 degree oven about 20 minutes.

Yield: 4 dozen rolls
Mrs. Helene Thawley

FRENCH BREAD

4 cups flour
½ cup milk
1 cup water
1 package dry or 1 cake
    compressed yeast

¼ cup warm water
1½ teaspoons shortening
1½ tablespoons sugar
2 teaspoons salt

Heat milk and 1 cup water to boiling. Remove from heat and cool to lukewarm. Sprinkle yeast over ¼ cup warm water until dissolved, then add to milk with shortening and ¾ tablespoon sugar. Sift flour into warm bowl with salt and remaining sugar, make a well in center and pour in yeast mixture. Stir thoroughly to mix, but do not knead. The dough will be soft. Cover with damp cloth and let rise for 2 hours or until doubled. Set oven at 400 degrees. Work dough lightly and turn out onto a floured board. Divide in half and pat each into 12x9 rectangle, roll up and continue rolling, tapering dough at ends to form a thin loaf that is approximately 15 inches long. Place loaves on greased baking sheet and cut diagonal shallow slits ½ inch deep across tops. Cover and let rise again in a warm place for 15-20 minutes or until almost double in size. Bake in heated oven with a pan of hot water placed in bottom of oven. (The steam from the pan of water insures a crisp crust). After 15 minutes reduce heat to 350 degrees and continue baking 30 minutes or until bread is crisp and brown. Cool on a wire rack.

Yield: 2 loaves
Barbara Maske

ZUCCHINI BREAD

1⅔ cups flour
¼ teaspoon baking powder
½ teaspoon salt
1½ cups sugar
1 teaspoon baking soda
½ teaspoon cinnamon
¼ teaspoon ground cloves

⅓ cup shortening
⅓ cup water
2 eggs (beaten)
1 cup zucchini squash, grated
½ cup raisins
½ cup nuts chopped

Stir until well blended. Pour into greased and floured 9x5x3-inch pan. Let stand 30 minutes to start action of baking powder. Bake at 350 degrees for 50-60 minutes. Cool 20 minutes. Remove from pan. Freezes well. (You may add 1 more cup of zucchini and leave out the raisins).

Yield: 1 loaf
Donna B. Kimball
Home Economics Extension Agent
for Caroline County

BUTTER FLAKES

1 cake bakers yeast
1 teaspoon salt
1½ teaspoons shortening
½ cup sugar

1 egg
3½ cups flour
2 tablespoons lukewarm water
1 cup hot water

Soften yeast in 2 tablespoons lukewarm water. To 1 cup hot water add salt, shortening and sugar. And cool. Add yeast and 1 beaten egg. Beat in flour and knead into a soft dough. Place in refrigerator. Remove 2 hours before serving. After 1 hour, roll dough to about ¼ inch thick, brush with melted butter. Cut in 2-inch strips, stack 5 high, then cut in 2-inch squares. Arrange in greased muffin pans. When double in bulk, bake same as any roll in 350 degree oven until tips are a nice brown—about 20 minutes.

Yield: 2 dozen rolls
Vera Van Schaik

CORN PONE

1 cup flour
1 teaspoon salt
1 teaspoon baking soda
3 tablespoons sugar

1 cup corn meal
3 tablespoons melted bacon
   drippings
2 cups plain yogurt

Grease and heat in oven a dark cookie sheet that has sides. Sift together flour, salt, sugar, and baking soda. Stir in corn meal, then yogurt and melted shortening. Pour into pan. Bake 35 minutes or until golden in 400 degree oven. Cut into pieces.

Yield: 12 to 16 pieces
Regina Mueller

SEASONED HOT DOG ROLLS OR SLICED BREAD

1 large package rolls or loaf,
   sliced
¼ pound margarine

1 teaspoon celery salt
1 teaspoon onion salt
1 teaspoon Worcestershire sauce

Melt all in butter, then dip rolls in ½ of it, or sprinkle over loaf bread. Arrange bread in pan, and sprinkle other half of mixture over it. Sprinkle with caraway seeds. Heat in 400 degree oven until browned.

Yield: 1 dozen
Louise Crouse

WILLIAMSBURG CORNMEAL GRIDDLE CAKES

2 eggs
1¼ cups buttermilk
1 tablespoon salad oil

1 cup yellow or white cornmeal
½ teaspoon baking soda
½ teaspoon salt

In medium bowl, beat eggs until frothy. Add buttermilk, oil, baking soda, and salt. Stir only until dry ingredients are moistened. Cook on hot greased griddle until brown on both sides.

Yield: 18 griddle cakes
Betty Fleetwood

PEANUT BUTTER BREAD

2 cups flour
3 tablespoons sugar
4 teaspoons baking powder
1 teaspoon salt

1 egg
¾ cup peanut butter
1½ cups milk

Sift four dry ingredients together. Beat egg, add peanut butter, blending thoroughly. Add milk. Add liquid to flour mixture, stirring only until flour disappears. Bake in 350 degree oven in a greased loaf pan. Delicious with butter or jelly.

Yield: 1 loaf
Michelle Lee Johnson

WHITE BREAD

2 cups hot water and milk
    (½ each)
2 tablespoons shortening
2 teaspoons salt

2 tablespoons sugar
2 yeast cakes
10 cups white flour

Soften yeast cakes in ¼ cup lukewarm water. Mix hot water and milk, sugar, shortening, and salt. Cool to lukewarm. Add yeast mixture. Add flour gradually until mixture forms ball which pulls away from sides of bowl. Turn onto floured board and knead 100 strokes or until elastic. Place in greased bowl, cover, allow to rise until doubled in bulk. Turn onto floured board. Knead again. Divide into 2 loaves. Let rise until doubled in bulk. Bake at 400 degrees for 10 minutes. Reduce heat to 350 degrees and bake 40 minutes. Cool on rack.

Yield: 2 loaves
Beth Adams

On the Eastern Shore of Maryland, persons with extraordinary healing powers were known as "high women" and "high men".

VIRGINIA'S ORANGE ROLLS

1 cup scalded milk
½ cup shortening
⅓ cup sugar
1 teaspoon salt
1 cake yeast
¼ cup warm water

2 well beaten eggs
¼ cup orange juice
2 tablespoons grated orange rind
4½ cups flour
2 tablespoons salad oil

Mix milk, sugar, salt, and shortening in large bowl. Add yeast dissolved in ¼ cup warm water. Add eggs, orange juice, and rind. Mix well. Add flour, leaving ½ cup flour for board. Mix well. Mold dough with the ½ cup on board. Knead. Brush bowl with salad oil. Place dough in bowl and brush lightly with oil. Cover with soft cloth, let rise until double in bulk. Punch down on floured board, knead well. Roll out dough to ¼ inch thickness, cut into long strips. To make figure 8s, cross strip over in center to make a figure 8, pinch ends together, and place on greased baking sheet. Cover and let rise again. Bake in 400 degree oven about 15 minutes. When ready to serve, drizzle mixture of orange juice and confectioner's sugar over rolls. These keep well; can be frozen.

Yield: 3 dozen rolls
Virginia Brown

LOCKSHERR KUGEL

1 box noodles cooked
¼ pound butter
½ cup milk
¼ pound cream cheese
½ pound cottage cheese
½ pint sour cream

2 teaspoons cinnamon
½ teaspoon salt
1 cup sugar
4 eggs
½ cup raisins
2 or 3 sliced apples

Mix all together. Bake 1½ hours in greased casserole at 300 degrees.

Yield: 8 to 10 servings
Mary Joyce Zeigler

B
R
E
A
D
S

THE MASTER MIX

For 13 cups

9 cups sifted all-purpose flour or 10 cups sifted soft wheat or cake flour
⅓ cup double-acting baking powder
1 tablespoon salt
¼ cup sugar
2 cups shortening which does not require refrigeration
1 cup dry milk

Product and Baking	Mix	Sugar	Milk	Eggs	Other Ingredients	Amount of Mixing
Biscuits (15-20) 450°-10 min.	3c		⅔ to 1c			Until blended Knead 15 strokes
(Hot griddle or iron) Griddle Cakes (18) or waffles (6)	3c	1c	1 ½c			Until blended
Muffins (12) 425°-20 min.	3c	2T	1c	1		Dry ingredients just moistened
Gingerbread (12) 350°-40 min.	2c	¼c	½c or H2o	1	½ c. molasses ½ tsp. cinnamon ½ tsp. ginger ½ tsp. cloves	Add liquid and beat 2 min. Other liquid, beat 1 min.
Oatmeal cookies 4 dozen 375° 10-12 min.	3c	1c	⅓c	1	1 tsp. cinnamon 1 cup quick rolled oats	Until blended
Drop cookies 4 dozen 375° 10-12 min.	3c	1c	⅓c	1	1 tsp. vanilla ½ cup nuts or chocolate bits	Until blended
Coffee Cake 400° 25 min.	3c	½c	⅔c	1	Topping; ½ cup brown sugar, 3T. butter ½ tsp. cinnamon	Until blended
Yellow Cake 375° 25 min.	3c	1 ¼c	1c	2	1 tsp. vanilla	2 min. after ⅔ liquid; 2 min. after ⅓ liquid
Chocolate Cake 375° 25 min.	3c	1 ½c	1c	2	1 tsp. vanilla ½ cup cocoa	2 min. after ⅔ liquid; 2 min. after ⅓ liquid

University of Maryland
Cooperative Extension Service

ZUCCHINI BREAD

3 eggs
2 cups sugar
1 cup salad oil
1 teaspoon vanilla
3 cups unsifted flour
1 teaspoon salt

1 teaspoon baking soda
2 teaspoons cinnamon
1½ cups chopped walnuts or
   raisins
3 cups grated raw zucchini
   (peeled and seeded)

Mix together everything except the zucchini. The batter will be stiff. Then add the zucchini. Pour into two greased loaf pans and bake 1 hour at 350 degrees.

Yield: 2 loaves
W. Henry Thomas
House of Delegates
Annapolis, Md.

KOLACHKY

1 yeast cake
½ cup milk
½ teaspoon salt

4 tablespoons melted butter
2¾ cups sifted flour

Crumble yeast into lukewarm milk, add salt, melted butter (cooled). Add flour and milk to make a stiff dough. Place in greased pan. Allow to double in bulk. Roll out to ½-inch thickness, cut into circles.

Make a depression in center of each circle. Fill with cheese spread. Bake at 375 degrees about ½ hour.

Apricot or prune filling may be substituted.

Yield: 12 servings
Beth Adams

If you eat the last piece of food on the plate you'll be an old maid.

STRAWBERRY BREAD

3 cups flour
1 teaspoon soda
1 teaspoon salt
1 tablespoon cinnamon
2 cups sugar

4 beaten eggs
1¼ cups vegetable oil
2 cups thawed strawberries
1¼ cups chopped nuts

Combine dry ingredients. Add eggs, oil, drained strawberries, and nuts. Stir just to moisten and mix. Spoon batter into 2 greased 9x5x3-inch loaf pans. Bake at 350 degrees for 50 to 70 minutes.

Yield: 2 loaves
Sonya Felipe

SPOON ROLLS

1 package active dry yeast
2 cups warm water
½ cup shortening (scant)
¼ cup granulated sugar

1 egg
2 teaspoons salt
4 cups flour

Place yeast in warm water, stir to dissolve. Set aside. Melt shortening. Cream shortening with sugar and salt. Add beaten egg. Add dissolved yeast and flour. Stir until well mixed. To bake, drop by spoon into well greased muffin tins. Bake at 450 degrees 15 to 20 minutes.

Yield: 2 dozen rolls
Kay Howell

PUMPKIN BREAD

⅔ cup vegetable shortening
3 cups sugar
4 eggs
2 cups mashed, cooked pumpkin
⅔ cup cold water

2⅔ cups flour
2 teaspoons soda
1 teaspoon baking powder
1 teaspoon ground cloves
1 teaspoon cinnamon

Mix all ingredients together well. Put in greased floured pan and bake. I always fit a piece of brown shopping bag in the bottom of the cake pan before greasing. Use tube pan or 2 loaf pans. You may add other spices according to taste. Maybe a little allspice, nutmeg, ginger, etc. Bake at 350 degrees for 1½ hours. You may also use your zucchini or butternut squash in place of pumpkin. Good at Christmas!

Yield: 2 loaves
Mrs. William Patchett

POPOVERS

Butter or margarine
4 eggs
1½ cups milk
¼ cup butter or margarine,
    melted

1¼ cups flour (sift before
    measuring)
½ teaspoon salt

Preheat oven to 400 degrees. Grease well, 8 custard cups with butter. Beat eggs well, then beat in milk and melted butter. Sift flour with salt; beat into egg mixture until smooth. Pour into prepared custard cups, placed not too close together, on a large cookie sheet. Bake 50 minutes. Serve hot.

Yield: 8 servings
Kay Howell

BUBBLE BREAD

1 package frozen Parker House
   rolls
1 4-ounce package butterscotch
   pudding (not instant)

1 stick melted butter
Cinnamon (lots!)
½ cup brown sugar
½ cup chopped nuts (any kind)

Butter Bundt pan. Arrange rolls in bottom. Pour melted butter over. Sprinkle with pudding, then cinnamon. Sprinkle on brown sugar and nuts. Let stand 8 hours or overnight. Bake at 350 degrees for 25 minutes. Let stand 5 minutes. Invert on plate.

Yield: 1 pan
Kay Everngam

GOOD HONEY WHEAT BREAD

2 packages dry yeast
2 cups warm water
¼ cup soy flour
3½ cups whole wheat flour

¼ cup oil
1½ tablespoons salt
½ cup honey
1½ cups white flour

In mixing bowl soften yeast in water. When bubbly, add soy flour, 1½ cups wheat flour, oil, salt, honey. Add white flour. Beat until smooth. Mix in rest of whole wheat flour. Knead 10 minutes. Let rise until double in bulk. Punch down and shape in loaves, in greased loaf pans. Let rise until double in bulk. Bake at 350 degrees 35 to 45 minutes.

Yield: 2 loaves
Virginia Brown

MOTHER'S SWEET RUSKS

⅔ cup shortening
⅔ cup sugar
1½ teaspoons salt
1 cup mashed potatoes

1 cake yeast
1½ cups lukewarm water
7½ cups flour
3 beaten eggs

Mix together and add 3 beaten eggs. Add 1 cake yeast dissolved in ½ cup lukewarm water. Add alternately, 1 cup lukewarm water and 7½ cups flour. More flour is needed if made of spring wheat. Roll out and shape as any kind of roll. Allow to rise and bake at 400 degrees for 20 minutes or until lightly browned.

Yield: 3 to 4 dozen
Mary Shawn Horsey

HOT CROSS BUNS

1 cup scalded milk
¾ teaspoon salt
½ cup sugar
½ cup shortening
1 teaspoon nutmeg

1 yeast cake softened in ¼
    cup warm water
4½ cups flour (about)
3 egg yolks

Add scalded milk to salt, sugar, nutmeg, and shortening. When lukewarm, add yeast and one and one-half cups flour. Beat well and let rise unil very light. Add the egg yolks and the remaining flour. Knead lightly and let rise until double in bulk. [Roll out dough to one inch thickness and cut into rounds, or form the dough into buns). Set close together on a greased pan and let rise. Glaze the surface of each bun with a little egg white diluted with water. With a sharp knife cut a cross on top of each bun. Bake about twenty minutes in a hot oven (400 degrees). Just before removing from the oven, brush with sugar and water. Fill the cross with a plain frosting. A cup of raisins may be added to the dough, if desired.

Yield: 2½ dozen
Mrs. Helene Thawley

Salads were most likely to be lettuce, radishes, cucumbers, spring onions and tomatoes, often enjoyed on a family picnic.

SALADS
and
SALAD
DRESSINGS

CHICKEN PECAN SALAD

3 medium peaches (1½ cups)
   peeled, and sliced
3 cups cubed cooked chicken
1 cup diced celery
½ teaspoon salt

½ cup mayonnaise
2 tablespoons salad oil
1 tablespoon vinegar
¼ cup toasted broken pecans

Reserve a few peach slices for garnish.

In a large bowl, combine cut up peaches, chicken and celery. Blend together next 4 ingredients. Toss with chicken mixture. Chill. Fold in nuts. Serve in Cranberry Ring.

CRANBERRY RING

2 3-ounce packages lemon gelatin
¼ teaspoon salt
2 cups orange juice

1 cup water
1 16-ounce can whole cranberry
   sauce

Mix gelatin, salt, water, and 1 cup orange juice until dissolved. Heat to boiling. Stir in 1 cup cold orange juice. Chill until partially set. Stir in cranberry sauce. Pour into 6½ cup ring mold. Chill until firm.

Yield: 6 to 8 servings
Edna E. Parrish

RED BEET EGGS

1 16-ounce can beets
1 cup vinegar
¾ cup sugar
1 tablespoon salt
1 tablespoon mixed pickling
   spices

6 hard-cooked eggs
1 medium onion, thinly sliced
   and separated into rings

Drain beets, reserving liquid. Pour liquid into a glass jar or bowl. Add vinegar, sugar, salt, and spices. Stir until sugar dissolves. Add beets, eggs, and onion. Cover. Chill two hours or longer.

Yield: 6 eggs
Marianne Kent

CHERRY SALAD SUPREME

1 3-ounce package raspberry
   gelatin
1 21-ounce can cherry pie filling
1 3-ounce package lemon gelatin
1 3-ounce package cream cheese
⅓ cup salad dressing

1 8¾-ounce can or 1 cup
   crushed pineapple
½ cup whipping cream
1 cup miniature marshmallows
2 tablespoons chopped nuts
2 cups boiling water

Dissolve raspberry gelatin in 1 cup boiling water. Stir in pie filling. Turn
into 9x9-inch pan and chill until partially set. Dissolve lemon gelatin in 1
cup boiling water. Beat together cream cheese and salad dressing.
Gradually add lemon gelatin. Stir in undrained pineapple. Whip ½ cup
whipping cream and fold into lemon mixture, with 1 cup miniature
marshmallows. Spread on top of cherry gelatin layer. Top with 2 tablespoons chopped nuts. Chill well.

Yield: 12 servings
Hazel Carey

DANDELION SALAD

1½ pounds dandelion greens
¼ pound bacon sliced
¾ cup light cream
3 eggs, beaten

1 tablespoon granulated sugar
⅓ cup cider vinegar
1 teaspoon salt
1 teaspoon paprika

Wash and trim dandelion greens, drain, and place in salad bowl. Fry
bacon till crisp, cut up, remove bits, and drain off all but 3 tablespoons
bacon fat. Add cream and blend. Beat eggs with sugar, vinegar, salt, and
paprika. Stir slowly into cream mix. Cook over low heat, stirring constantly till slightly thickened. Pour hot dressing over dandelion greens,
and toss. Sprinkle with bacon bits. Good with chilled dry white wine.

Yield: 6 servings
Florence Howard

CHICKEN SALAD NOEL

2 cups cooked, cubed chicken
¼ cup chopped onion
1 cup drained pineapple chunks

1 cup sliced celery
½ cup sliced water chestnuts
2 tablespoons currants (dried)

DRESSING

1 cup mayonnaise
¼ cup sour cream
2 tablespoons lemon juice

½ teaspoon curry powder
¼ cup chutney
½ cup almonds

Toss chicken, onion, pineapple, celery, chestnuts, and currants together. Mix dressing well and pour over salad. The salad is better if flavors are allowed to meld before serving.

Yield: 6 servings
Beth Adams

CRANBERRY SALAD OR DESSERT

1 pound cranberries, washed, drained, and ground
1 tablespoon orange concentrate
1½ cups sugar
1 #2 can crushed pineapple, drained (reserve juice for something else)

1 cup white grapes, chopped, and seeds removed
1 cup chopped nuts
1 package whipped topping
4 or 5 cups of tiny marshmallows

Grind cranberries or chop (too fine will be juicy, too coarse will be sour and tart). Add sugar and concentrate; stir until sugar dissolves. Add pineapple, whipped topping, nuts, grapes, and marshmallows. Keeps well about a week.

Yield: 12 servings
Mary Wharton

HOLIDAY CRANBERRY SALAD

1 pound cranberries
1¾ cups water
2 3-ounce packages cherry gelatin
½ cup sugar
1 cup Tokay grapes
1 cup finely chopped celery

1 #2 can crushed pineapple
1 3-ounce package cream cheese
16 large marshmallows, quartered
1 cup whipping cream
Crisp salad greens

Wash cranberries. Add water and cook until they start to pop. Boil 5 minutes. Beat with a rotary beater to break up berries. Add gelatin and sugar and stir until dissolved. Place over ice water and stir frequently until thick. Cut grapes in half, and remove seeds. Fold into jellied mixture with celery and undrained pineapple. Pour into large ring mold and refrigerate over night. Mash cheese in a bowl. Add marshmallows and cream and place in refrigerator over night. Beat with electric mixer until stiff. Place mold on salad greens and serve with cream mixture.

Yield: 12 servings
Edna E. Parrish

FROZEN COLESLAW

3 medium to large heads of
    cabbage
3 chopped green sweet peppers
3 chopped red sweet peppers

3 chopped medium onions
3 heaping tablespoons salt
4½ cups water

Sprinkle the cabbage, peppers and onions with the salt and cover with 4½ cups of boiling water. Let stand one hour. Drain thoroughly and cover with syrup.

SYRUP

5½ cups sugar
3½ cups vinegar

¾ cup water
3 teaspoons celery seed

Dissolve all ingredients together. Mix slaw well with syrup and freeze. Serve slaw only partially thawed.

Yield: 8 pints
Virginia Warren

HOT COLD SLAW

S
A
L
A
D
S

2 medium heads of cabbage   2 tablespoons of salt
2 medium onions

Shred cabbage and place in refrigerator pan. Cover with layer of onions, sliced paper thin. Sprinkle with salt.

DRESSING

1 cup salad oil   1 teaspoon salt
1 cup vinegar   1 teaspoon dry mustard
2 tablespoons celery seed   7/8 cup sugar

Bring dressing ingredients to a rolling boil. While dressing is boiling hot, pour over cabbage and onions. Allow to set for 24 hours, covered. Mix vigorously and it is ready to serve. May be refrigerated for several days.

Yield: 16 to 20 servings
Lois Pelosky

KIDNEY BEAN SALAD

1 can kidney beans, rinsed and   2 small onions—chopped fine
    drained   1 large sour pickle, chopped fine
2 cups finely shredded cabbage

Have vegetables chilled and mix with dressing below. Mix way ahead of time to use so flavors will permeate.

DRESSING FOR KIDNEY BEAN SALAD

¾ cup apple cider vinegar   1 egg
¼ cup water   Salt to taste
½ cup sugar

Beat egg in sauce pan, add sugar, then vinegar and salt. Place over medium heat and cook until it "boils up good." Cool and refrigerate before using. (Better to make day before you serve salad).

Yield: 8 servings
R. Doris Stivers

JOYCE'S CREAMED CUCUMBER WHEELS

1 large cucumber
½ cup sour cream
½ teaspoon salt

¼ cup sugar
2 tablespoons vinegar

Wash cucumber. With tines of fork score cucumber lengthwise. Slice crosswise to make wheels. Set aside. Combine sour cream, salt, sugar, and vinegar. Mix thoroughly. Add cucumber wheels. Cover and refrigerate several hours.

Yield: 4 to 5 servings
Joyce Lorraine Johnson

ITALIAN SALAD

1 pound box shell macaroni
¼ pound hard salami
¼ pound Provolone cheese
¼ pound pepperoni
3 green peppers

1 small jar mushrooms
2 sticks celery
3 tomatoes
1 small jar olives

Cook macaroni. Chop all other ingredients and add to macaroni.

DRESSING

⅔ cup oil
1 teaspoon salt
1 teaspoon oregano

½ cup vinegar
½ teaspoon pepper

Toss salad lightly with dressing. Refrigerate.

Yield: 8 to 10 servings
Lynnette Scanga

MACARONI AND CHEESE SALAD

6 ounces shell macaroni (1½ cups)
1 cup sliced celery
1 cup shredded carrot
¼ cup chopped onion
1 can Cheddar cheese soup
Dash pepper

¼ cup cooking oil
2 tablespoons vinegar
1 teaspoon sugar
1 teaspoon prepared mustard
1 teaspoon Worcestershire sauce
½ teaspoon salt

Cook macaroni according to package directions; drain and cool. Combine macaroni, celery, carrot, and onion. In small mixer bowl combine soup, oil, vinegar, sugar, mustard, Worcestershire sauce, salt, and pepper. Beat until well blended. Spoon atop macaroni mixture. Mix well. Chill several hours.

Yield: 4 to 6 servings
Regina S. Mueller

SHRIMP MACARONI SALAD

3 cans (4½ or 5-ounce) shrimp
2 cups cooked elbow macaroni
1 cup chopped raw cauliflower
1 cup sliced celery
¼ cup chopped parsley
¼ cup chopped sweet pickle
½ cup mayonnaise or salad
    dressing
3 tablespoons garlic french
    dressing

1 tablespoon lemon juice
1 teaspoon grated onion
1 teaspoon celery seed
1 teaspoon salt
¼ teaspoon pepper
Salad greens
1 hard-cooked egg, sliced

Drain shrimp. Cover with ice water and let stand five minutes. Drain. Cut large shrimp. Combine macaroni, cauliflower, celery, parsley, pickle, and shrimp. Combine dressings, lemon juice, onion, and seasonings. Mix well. Add mayonnaise mixture to shrimp mixture. Toss lightly; chill. Serve on salad greens. Garnish with egg slices.

Yield: 6 servings
Nellie Dean

ORANGE SHERBET SALAD OR DESSERT

2 3-ounce packages orange
    gelatin
1 cup boiling water
1 pint orange sherbet

1 cup whipping cream
1 small can Mandarin oranges,
    drained
1 cup finely chopped nuts

Dissolve gelatin in water. Add orange sherbet. Stir until dissolved. Fold in whipped cream; add oranges. Add nuts, reserving a portion to garnish the top. Pour into lightly oiled 1½-quart ring mold. Chill until firm.

Yield: 4 to 6 servings
Mary Shawn Horsey

RECEPTION SALAD

1 package lime, orange, or lemon
    gelatin
1 (8-ounce) package cream cheese
1 large can crushed pineapple
1 small jar pimento

½ cup chopped walnuts
½ cup chopped celery
1 cup whipping cream, whipped
⅛ teaspoon salt

Dissolve gelatin in heated pineapple juice. Soften the cream cheese and mash with the chopped pimentos. When gelatin starts to jell, fold in: pineapple, cream cheese, celery, nuts, whipped cream and salt. Chill until firm.

Note: Cottage cheese may be used instead of cream cheese for fewer calories.

Yield: 12 servings
Mary McHarry

HOT POTATO SALAD (PENNSYLVANIA DUTCH)

4 slices diced bacon
½ cup chopped onion
2 hard-cooked eggs
1 quart hot cooked potatoes
¼ cup vinegar

1 egg
1 tablespoon sugar
Salt and pepper to taste
2 tablespoons chopped parsley

Dice bacon and fry. Add vinegar, salt, pepper, sugar and beaten egg, and cook slightly. Pour mixture over hot cubed potatoes. Mix in onion and sliced hard boiled eggs. Sprinkle with chopped parsley. Blend lightly and serve hot.

Yield: 10-12 servings
Jane (Johnson) States

GREAT GRANDMA LUCY'S POTATO SALAD

10 to 12 medium potatoes
3 slices of bacon
¼ cup vinegar
1 tablespoon sugar
1 teaspoon salt
1 onion (diced)
1 cup celery (diced)

Celery seed
Green pepper (optional)
½ teaspoon mustard
1 cup mayonnaise
Cherry tomatoes or tomato
  wedges

Wash and cook potatoes in their skins. Barely cover with cold water and simmer until they test done with a fork. Spread on a large platter to cool. Gently scrape off skins and remove any blemishes. Slice into pieces desired for salad. Cook 3 slices of bacon until crisp and break into small pieces. Pour pieces and grease over potato pieces. Make up a mixture of the vinegar, sugar, and salt and pour evenly over potatoes. Add onion, celery, celery seed as desired, and finely diced green pepper. Add mustard and mayonnaise. Mix thoroughly. Garnish with cherry tomatoes or tomato wedges. Serve on a bed of lettuce leaves.

Yield: 8 to 10 servings
Rita Rogers Kearney

STRAWBERRY SALAD

1 package (10-ounce) strawberries,
  thawed
½ cup boiling water
1 package (3-ounce) strawberry
  gelatin

1 small can crushed pineapple
½ cup nuts, chopped
½ pint sour cream

Dissolve gelatin in boiling water. Let cool. Add strawberries. Stir and add pineapple and nuts. Put half of mixture in pan and congeal. Spread sour cream. Then pour remaining gelatin mix, making 3 layers. Return to refrigerator to jell.

Yield: 12 servings
Florence F. Nuttle

STRAWBERRY SOUR CREAM SALAD

2 packages (6-ounce) strawberry
  gelatin
2 cups boiling water
2 (10-ounce) packages frozen
  strawberries, thawed

2 medium bananas, mashed
1 cup chopped nuts
1 pint dairy sour cream

Dissolve gelatin in boiling water. Add all ingredients except sour cream. Pour one half mixture into mold. Let chill one hour. Spread sour cream over gelatin in mold and spoon remaining mixture over top. Chill.

Yield: 8-10 servings
Sonya Felipe

SAUERKRAUT SALAD

1 large can sauerkraut (rinse well)	1½ cups sugar
1 green pepper	½ cup oil
1 large onion	⅔ cup vinegar
1 cup celery	½ cup water

Chop sauerkraut, pepper, onion, and celery in small pieces. Mix sugar, oil, vinegar, and water; then add other ingredients. Mix well and refrigerate for 12 hours.

Yield: 12 servings
Pauline Luff

SPINACH SALAD

1 pound young, tender, fresh spinach, washed and drained	3 hard-cooked eggs, finely chopped
1 small can water chestnuts, drained and sliced	6 slices crisp bacon, drained and crumbled
½ pound fresh mushrooms, washed and sliced	

Tear spinach into bite-sized pieces and toss with mushrooms and water chestnuts. Add the following dressing.

DRESSING

¼ cup salad oil	1 tablespoon sugar
¼ cup vinegar	1 teaspoon salt
½ cup catsup	

Mix with chopped eggs and crumbled bacon.

Yield: 6 servings
Jane B. Crouse
Extension Agent, Home Economics
Kent County

ORANGE NUT SALAD

4 oranges   Chopped nuts
1 8-ounce package cream cheese

Peel 4 oranges and slice ¼ inch thick. Place on lettuce. Divide one 8-ounce package cream cheese into 8 pieces, form into balls. Roll in finely chopped nuts. Add to salad. Serve with French Dressing.

Yield: 4 servings
Kay Howell

"I've been fixin' to"—precedes many a statement made by procrastinators on the Eastern Shore.

PEAR SALAD

1 package lime gelatin   1 8-ounce can evaporated milk
1 8-ounce package cream cheese   (chill in ice box)
1 #2 can of pears

Drain pears. Heat 1 cup juice from the pears. Dissolve lime gelatin and chill until like syrup. Mash pears and cream cheese. Add whipped milk. Pour into 8x12-inch pan or 9-inch. Chill. Cut in squares.

Yield: 9-12 servings
Florence F. Nuttle

TABBOULEH

1 cup uncooked bulghur (cracked
  wheat)
½ cup olive oil
½ cup lemon juice
1 cup finely chopped green onion
1 cup chopped celery
1 cup chopped parsley

1 cup chopped fresh mint or
  2 tablespoons dried mint
3 ripe tomatoes, chopped
2 teaspoons salt
2 grindings black pepper
2 large cucumbers

Using a two quart jar with tight fitting lid, place bulghur in bottom of
jar. Beat oil and lemon juice and pour over the bulghur. Layer each
vegetable in order named over the bulghur as listed, ending with
cucumber, peeled, seeded, and chopped Sprinkle with salt and pepper.
Cover container and refrigerate for 24 hours. Just before serving, toss
the salad to mix ingredients.

Yield: 2 quarts
Carol Stockley

FROZEN PINEAPPLE SALAD

1 pint dairy sour cream
2 tablespoons lemon juice
⅛ teaspoon salt
1 (8 or 9-ounce) can crushed
  pineapple, well drained

¼ cup chopped maraschino
  cherries (optional)
¾ cup sugar
¼ cup chopped walnuts
1 banana, sliced

Mix sour cream, juice, salt, and sugar. Add remaining ingredients.
Blend. Pour into medium-sized muffin tins lined with paper cups. Freeze
until firm. Remove papers to serve.

Yield: 10 medium salads
Sonya Felipe

CAROLINE COUNTY SALAD DRESSING

2 eggs
¾ cup sugar
Dash red pepper
1 tablespoon butter

Pinch salt
1 teaspoon dry mustard
½ cup vinegar

Mix, then stir, cooking until thick, about five minutes. Chill. Good on slaw or salads.

Yield: 1½ cups
Florence F. Nuttle

SLAW SALAD DRESSING

2 eggs beaten
½ teaspoon salt
½ teaspoon mustard
1 tablespoon cornstarch

6 tablespoons sugar
6 tablespoons vinegar
Enough water to make cup
Butter (1-2 tablespoons)

Mix together and add the butter after it is cooked or comes to a boil. Chill.

Yield: 1½ cups
Florence F. Nuttle

LOW CALORIE LEMON FRENCH DRESSING

1 teaspoon unflavored gelatin
1 tablespoon cold water
¼ cup boiling water
2 to 3 tablespoons sugar
½ teaspoon salt
1 teaspoon grated lemon peel

½ cup fresh lemon juice
¼ teaspoon garlic salt
⅛ teaspoon pepper
⅛ teaspoon dry mustard
¼ teaspoon Worcestershire sauce

Soften gelatin in cold water. Add boiling water and stir until gelatin dissolves. Stir in sugar and salt until dissolved. Combine mixture with remaining ingredients in a container with a tight fitting lid; shake well. Serve cool, but not chilled, over crisp salad greens. May be covered and stored in refrigerator until needed. If refrigerated before serving, place container of dressing in pan of hot water for 5 minutes to reliquify the gelatin. One tablespoon: 12 to 13 calories.

Yield: 1 cup
Sara Kidd

ZIPPY SALAD DRESSING
Fat Free

1 tablespoon or less chopped
   onion
½ teaspoon green pepper
   (optional)
¼ cup chopped raw carrots
1 teaspoon finely chopped
   parsley

¼ teaspoon non-caloric sweetener
1 cup of tomato juice
¼ cup vinegar
Salt and pepper to taste

Chop all vegetables finely. Combine ingredients in a jar with tightly fitted top. Shake until blended. Refrigerate covered and shake well before using.

Yield: 1¾ cups
2 tablespoons—6 calories
Sara Kidd

MY OWN SALAD DRESSING

Mixture #1

1 cup sugar	1 teaspoon dry mustard
1 teaspoon celery seed	1 teaspoon salt
Dash of pepper	½ cup vinegar
½ cup water	1 tablespoon butter

Stir together and bring to boil on medium fire. Remove from heat.

Mixture #2

3 eggs beaten	1 cup milk
1 tablespoon cornstarch dissolved in ½ cup milk	

Slowly stir mixture #1 into mixture #2, mixing briskly all the while. Return to fire and stir until thickened. One cup of commercial mayonnaise may be beaten in. Especially good for potato salad, cole slaw or vegetable salads.

Yield: 1 quart
Mary Shawn Horsey

BOILED DRESSING FOR CHICKEN SALAD

½ cup plus 1 tablespoon sugar	¾ cup water
¼ cup plus 2 tablespoons flour	1 cup milk
¾ tablespoon salt	2 tablespoons butter
¾ tablespoon dry mustard	¼ cup mayonnaise
4 eggs	Cayenne pepper
¾ cup vinegar	

Mix sugar, flour, salt and mustard. Beat eggs. Add beaten eggs, vinegar, and water to dry ingredients. Cook over medium heat, stirring constantly, until thickened. Use electric mixer if lumpy. When it starts to thicken, add milk and butter. Continue cooking and stirring until thick. Remove from heat. Add mayonnaise and cayenne.

Yield: 1 quart
Kay Everngam

BLUE CHEESE DRESSING

1 cup salad oil
½ cup cider vinegar
½ cup water
1 teaspoon garlic salt
1 teaspoon parsley flakes

2 tablespoons sugar
1 tablespoon minced onion
4-ounce package blue cheese,
  crumbled

Put ingredients in shaker bottle. Shake well.

Yield: 2½ cups
Carol Stockley

CENTURY OLD FRENCH DRESSING

½ cup sugar
1 cup water
½ cup lemon juice
½ cup vinegar (scant)
2 cups olive oil

½ teaspoon salt
2 teaspoons celery salt
1 large onion grated very fine
½ teaspoon white pepper
1 cup catsup

Boil sugar and water 10 minutes. Add lemon juice and boil five minutes more. Cool. Mix salts and pepper and stir into vinegar. Add oil and all remaining ingredients. Shake well before using.

Yield: 6¼ cups
Given to Ruth G. Jones by
Alice B. Walker in the late 1930's

Although the traditional Eastern Shore fishing boats no longer sail up the Choptank, the vessels in this turn of the century photograph are docked at Denton, Caroline's County Seat.

SEAFOODS

MARYLAND LADY CRAB CAKES

1 pound Maryland crabmeat
1 cup Italian seasoned bread
   crumbs
1 large egg (or 2 small)
About ¼ cup mayonnaise
1 teaspoon Worcestershire sauce

1 teaspoon dry mustard
½ teaspoon salt
¼ teaspoon pepper
Margarine, butter or oil for
   frying

Remove all cartilage from crabmeat.

In a bowl, mix bread crumbs, egg, mayonnaise and seasonings. Add crab meat and mix gently but thoroughly. If mixture is too dry, add a little more mayonnaise. Shape into 6 cakes.

Cook cakes in fry pan, in just enough fat to prevent sticking, until browned; about 5 minutes on each side.

Note: If desired, crab cakes may be deep fried at 350 degrees 2 to 3 minutes, or until browned.

Yield: 6 crab cakes
Governor Harry R. Hughes
State of Maryland
Annapolis, Md.

CLAM QUICHE

1 unbaked pie shell, pricked
½ pound bacon, cooked and
   crumbled
1 15-ounce can clam chowder
4 eggs, slightly beaten

½ cup finely chopped onion
½ cup sour cream
2 tablespoons chopped parsley
¼ teaspoon pepper
4 slices cheese

Preheat oven to 400 degrees. Bake pie shell 8 minutes and remove. Reduce heat to 325 degrees. In bowl, combine bacon, chowder, eggs, onion, sour cream, parsley, pepper. Mix well. Pour about ⅔ mixture into shell. Arrange cheese on top. Top with rest of chowder mixture. Bake 50 to 55 minutes or until set. Let stand 20 minutes before cutting.

Yield:: 5 to 6 servings
Dorothy Brown

CLAM SAUCE FOR SPAGHETTI OR SHELL MACARONI

¼ cup olive oil or vegetable oil
3 tablespoons butter
1 large clove of garlic, minced
2 8-ounce cans minced clams

½ cup chopped parsley
¼ teaspoon pepper
1 pound spaghetti or macaroni

Heat butter, oil, and minced garlic, sauté until garlic is golden. Drain clam juice into butter mixture, add pepper and simmer 10 minutes. Add clams and ¼ cup of chopped parsley. Heat through. Drain spaghetti or shells that have been cooked according to package directions. Mix one cup of sauce with spaghetti or shells, then top with remaining sauce. Garnish with remaining parsley. Serve with Parmesan cheese. Sauce may be made ahead. Refrigerate and reheat at serving time.

Yield: 8 servings
Regina Mueller

CRAB IMPERIAL

1 pound crab meat
4 tablespoons mayonnaise
¾ teaspoon Worcestershire sauce
¼ teaspoon salt
Dash of Louisiana Hot Sauce

Pinch each of thyme, oregano,
dry mustard, and
monosodium glutamate
1 egg

Mix all ingredients, adding crab meat last. Coat a casserole lightly with mayonnaise and fill with crab mixture. Spread a thin layer of mayonnaise over top and sprinkle with paprika and parsley. Bake at 350 degrees for 35 to 40 minutes.

Yield: 4 servings
Tidewater Inn
Easton, Md.

CRAB CAKES

1 pound fresh crabmeat, drained
    and flaked
½ to ¾ cup mayonnaise
½ cup fine dry breadcrumbs
1 egg, beaten

1 teaspoon prepared mustard
¾ to 1 teaspoon white pepper
    (optional)
¼ teaspoon parsley flakes
Pinch of salt

Combine all ingredients; stir well. Shape mixture into 10 patties. Fry in deep hot oil (375 degrees) until patties are golden brown. Drain on paper towels.

Yield: 10 (2-inch) patties
Town Creek Restaurant & Marina
Oxford, Maryland

CRAB CAKES

1 pound crab meat
1 egg beaten
2 rolls for crumbs (or 2 or 3
    slices stale bread)
Minced onion

Parsley
Salt
Cayenne pepper
Pepper to taste
Prepared mustard (optional)

Mix all together. If too dry, add milk. Form into cakes and brown slowly.

Yield: 6 to 8 cakes
Kay Howell

CRAB CAKES

1 pound crabmeat
½ cup mayonnaise
1 tablespoon mustard

1 teaspoon Worcestershire sauce
1 egg
½ cup cracker crumbs (crushed)

Mix well, form into six patties and fry.

Yield: 6 patties
Ginny Watson

CRAB IMPERIAL

1 large green pepper (1 cup diced)
2 pimentos, diced
1 tablespoon English mustard
1 tablespoon salt
½ teaspoon white pepper

2 eggs
1 cup mayonnaise
3 pounds backfin crabmeat
Mayonnaise for topping

Mix all ingredients except crabmeat. Add crabmeat lightly; put in shells or casserole. Top lightly with mayonnaise. Sprinkle with paprika. Bake at 350 degrees for 20-25 minutes.

Yield: 12-16 servings
Kay Everngam

CRAB IMPERIAL

1 pound crab backfin
1 ounce pimento, chopped
¾ cup mayonnaise
1 tablespoon mustard

2 tablespoons Worcestershire
1 teaspoon hot sauce or hot
  pepper sauce
2 tablespoons lemon juice

Mix all ingredients except crabmeat until smooth. Fold crabmeat in carefully, so as not to break. Bake 30 minutes at 350 degrees.

Yield: 6 to 8 servings
"Butterfly"

CRAB IMPERIAL

4 tablespoons butter
4 tablespoons flour
2 cups milk
1 teaspoon salt
¼ teaspoon black pepper
½ teaspoon celery salt
Dash cayenne
1 egg yolk, beaten

2 tablespoons sherry
1 cup soft bread crumbs
1 pound crab flakes
1 teaspoon minced parsley
1 teaspoon minced onion
¼ cup buttered crumbs
Paprika

Melt butter, add flour, blend, gradually add milk and seasonings. Cook over low heat. Gradually add yolk and cook 2 minutes longer. Take off heat and add sherry and bread crumbs. Mix, pour in well-greased casserole. Bake in hot oven 20 minutes.

Yield: 1 casserole
Carter M. Hickman

CRAB NORFOLK

1 pound crabmeat	Salt
¼ pound butter	Pepper
1½ tablespoons white wine	Red pepper to taste

Mix crab with seasonings, dot with butter, cover. Bake 20 to 30 minutes in 350 degree oven.

Yield: 6 to 8 servings
Dorothy Brown

CRAB-SHRIMP CASSEROLE

1 can crabmeat (1 pound)	1 teaspoon dry parsley
2 pounds shrimp	1 cup tomato juice
½ green pepper (chopped)	1 cup mayonnaise
½ cup chopped onion	1 tablespoon Worcestershire
2 cups cooked rice	sauce
1 small can mushrooms	½ cup milk
1 teaspoon salt	1 egg

Combine crabmeat, shrimp, pepper, onion, cooked rice, and mushrooms in large bowl, set aside. Combine tomato juice, mayonnaise, milk, Worcestershire sauce, egg, salt, and dried parsley in small bowl, pour over mixture in large bowl, put into 13x9-inch glass dish and cook uncovered in 325 degree oven for 45 minutes. You can also make this casserole using either shrimp or crabmeat instead of both and have an entirely different taste.

Yield: 8 to 10 servings
Barbara Maske

MYRTLE'S CRAB IMPERIAL

¼ pound butter
2 tablespoons flour
1 cup whipping cream
1 pound flaked crab meat
1 teaspoon prepared mustard
½ teaspoon salt
1 teaspoon dry mustard

Dash of cayenne pepper
2 tablespoons mayonnaise
1 teaspoon Worcestershire sauce
2 hard cooked eggs
1 medium pimento
Bread crumbs

Melt butter and blend in flour. Add whipping cream and stir and cook until smooth. Add crab meat, mustard, salt, dry mustard and pepper. Add mayonnaise, Worcestershire sauce, 2 finely chopped hard cooked eggs and pimento chopped. Blend well. Turn into casserole or crab shells and sprinkle with fine bread crumbs. Dot with butter and bake until heated through in 375 degree oven. You can use light cream and cut the butter to 4 tablespoons for a less rich imperial.

Yield: 8 servings
Myrtle Smith Hughes

CRAB IMPERIAL

1 pound crabmeat (backfin)
¼ cup mayonnaise
1 teaspoon horseradish (optional)
½ teaspoon salt
½ cup sour cream
1 teaspoon prepared mustard

1 tablespoon chopped parsley
2 tablespoons lemon juice
1 cup soft bread crumbs
¼ cup diced pimento
2 tablespoons capers (optional)

Mix all ingredients except crabmeat well. Gently fold in crabmeat. Bake in 2-quart casserole at 350 degrees for 20 to 25 minutes or until brown.

Yield: 6 to 8 servings
L. T. Short

CRAB FONDUE

1 pound crabmeat
1 8-ounce package cream cheese
1 6-ounce package Gruyere
    cheese, grated
½ cup milk
¼ teaspoon lemon pepper
    seasoning
¼ cup sherry

In fondue pot over low heat combine cheeses, milk, seasonings, and sherry. Stir until blended and smooth. Add crabmeat and stir until heated through. Serve with bread chunks. If mixture thickens, add extra milk or sherry.

Yield: 4 servings
Mark Adams

CLAMS ADAMO

½ cup margarine, melted
2 to 2½ tablespoons herbed
    bread crumbs
1 teaspoon lemon juice
2 tablespoons green onion,
    chopped
3 tablespoons slivered almonds,
    chopped
2 teaspoons anisette
2 teaspoons pimento, chopped
¼ teaspoon white pepper
½ teaspoon seafood seasoning
2 tablespoons parsley, chopped
1 pint hard shelled clams
    (quahogs) or oysters, shucked
Romano cheese, grated coarsely
Paprika

Blend together crumbs and margarine. Add lemon juice, onion, almonds, anisette, pimento, parsley, and spices. Drain clams. Cut clams or oysters into quarters or small pieces. Lay in bottom of buttered scallop shells or individual baking dishes. Cover with crumb mixture. Sprinkle with Romano cheese and paprika. Bake at 400 to 425 degrees until cheese melts and crumbs are browned, about 15 minutes.

Yield: 4 servings
Everett Adams

CLAM CAKES

1 egg
¼ cup milk
¾ cup clam juice
1 cup minced clams
1½ cups sifted flour

¼ teaspoon baking soda
½ teaspoon cream of tartar
¾ teaspoon salt
1 teaspoon baking powder

Beat eggs, add milk and clam juice. Sift together flour and remaining ingredients. Add to liquids and mix well. Add clams. Drop by spoonfuls into kettle of hot fat. Drain and serve hot with tartar sauce.

Yield: 4 servings
Gladys Whiting

CLAM FRITTERS

12 raw medium sized to large
   clams, minced
1 teaspoon chopped chives
2 tablespoons fine bread crumbs
2 tablespoons flour

¾ teaspoon baking powder
1 egg, beaten
¼ teaspoon salt
⅛ teaspoon pepper

Put all ingredients in a bowl and mix thoroughly. Drop by tablespoonsfull into deep hot fat and fry until lightly brown. Drain on brown paper or paper towels. Garnish with parsley and lemon wedge.

Yield: 8-10 fritters
Helen Thawley

"Lady, do you want some more arsters or are you all arstered up?" asked a waitress in an Eastern Shore seafood restaurant.

"MOM" KEARNEY'S SHRIMP CREOLE
1920 Maryland

3 slices bacon, diced
3 tablespoons chopped onion
2 tablespoons chopped celery
2 tablespoons chopped parsley
    (or ½ teaspoon parsley
    flakes)
3 tablespoons chopped green
    pepper

1 tablespoon flour
4 cups canned tomatoes
2 teaspoons salt
Few grains cayenne
Dash of chili powder
3 cups cooked rice
Cleaned shrimp broken into
    pieces

Fry bacon, add onion, celery, parsley, and green pepper. Cook, stirring until onion is yellow. Add flour and stir until slightly brown. Add tomatoes, salt, cayenne, and chili powder. Cover and cook slowly until thick, approximately 2 to 2½ hours. Add shrimp and heat through. Serve on rice.

Yield: 8 servings
Rita Rogers Kearney

SEAFOOD STEW

1 cup mixed seafood per person
1 cup medium cream per person

Butter

Suggested seafood mix—shrimp, scallops, lobster or crab, oysters. Cook shrimp and lobster, remove meat from shells. Cook scallops and oysters in a generous amount of butter until oysters begin to curl. Add lobster or crab and shrimp and heat thru. Add cream and heat slowly. Do not allow to boil. Ladle immediately into heated soup plates, top with paprika and serve. Very rich and requires only a salad as accompaniment. Do not double amounts. Make 2 separate batches if serving more than 4 people.

Yield: 4 servings
Beth Adams

SHRIMP MOLD

1 can tomato soup
1 (8-ounce) package of cream
    cheese
1½ tablespoons unflavored
    gelatin, diluted in ¼ cup
    water

1 cup finely chopped celery
¾ cup finely chopped scallions
1 cup mayonnaise
2 cans small shrimp or 1
    (8-ounce) package cooked
    frozen shrimp

Melt cream cheese in undiluted soup. Add gelatin and set aside to cool. Combine celery, scallions, shrimp and mayonnaise. When soup mixture is cool add to other ingredients. Pour mixure into greased mold and chill overnight.

Yield: 4-6 servings
Mrs. Barbara Maske

CAROLINE COUNTY SPRING SHAD STEW
A COLONIAL RECIPE

1 buck shad
2 teaspoons salt
½ teaspoon black pepper
1 bay leaf
1 hot red pepper pod
2 thick slices bacon

10 medium potatoes
6 medium onions, chopped
1 large turnip
4 cups water
2 cups dry white wine
1 quart milk

Clean shad and cut into pieces, with bone. Cover with 4 cups water; add bay leaf, salt and pepper pod and simmer until fish is tender. Drain and reserve liquid. Remove shad meat from bones and reserve meat. Cut bacon into small pieces and fry in large pot. Pare and dice potatoes and turnip. Add to bacon and fat in pot. Add chopped onion. Remove bay leaf and pepper pod from fish broth; add enough water to liquid to make 4 cups. Pour over vegetables and boil for 15 minutes. Add white wine and shad meat and simmer slowly for about one hour. Add the milk and stir constantly until the stew is heated thoroughly. Taste: add salt and pepper if needed. Serve very hot.

Yield: 12 to 15 servings
Max Chambers

BAKED FISH—VERONIQUE

1½ to 2 pounds fish fillets
1 cup dry white wine
1 cup seedless green grapes
   (halved)
½ cup cream with egg yolk
   beaten in

2 tablespoons butter
1½ tablespoons flour
2 to 4 tablespoons heavy cream
2 tablespoons slivered almonds

Sprinkle fish with paprika, pour wine over fish, bake at 325 degrees for 8 to 10 minutes. Baste 3 times. Reserve pan juices. Melt butter and blend in flour. Gradually add pan juices, should be about 1 cup. Stir and cook until smooth and begins to boil. Reduce heat, add cream and egg, salt and pepper to taste. Pour over fish. Arrange grapes on top. Place under broiler until bubbly. Dribble on 2 tablespoons of cream and sprinkle on almonds. Broil again until light brown.

Yield: 6 to 8 servings
Beth Adams

BAKED FISH

1½ to 2 pounds fish fillets
1 cup milk
1 tablespoon salt

1 cup crushed cracker crumbs
¼ cup melted butter

Mix milk and salt. Dip fish and roll in cracker crumbs. Place fish on cookie sheet and pour melted butter over all. Bake at 400 degrees about 15 minutes.

Yield: 6 to 8 servings
Dolly Moore

FISH FRY BATTER

1½ cups biscuit mix   1 egg
¾ cup beer   ¼ teaspoon salt

Beat together biscuit mix, beer, egg, and salt. Pat fish dry, dip in batter, fry in hot oil. A very light, crispy batter, also good for onion rings, or fruit fritters. Left over batter makes excellent crepes.

Yield: Enough batter for 2 pounds of fish and 1 quart of oysters
Mark Adams

BASIC FISH BATTER

1 egg yolk   ¾ cup self-rising flour
½ cup ice water   Shortening as desired

Beat egg yolk, add ice water, and beat again. Add flour and mix with spoon, but do not smooth mixture. Refrigerate batter for several hours. You may use a little fat in a skillet or a lot of fat in a deep fryer. Bring fat to bubbling. Then dip fish or seafood in batter and fry. It will be nice and crisp.

Yield: Enough for 1½ to 2 pounds fish
Dolly Moore

STUFFED FLOUNDER

1 medium to large baking fish or
    8 pieces of fillet of flounder
Salt
Pepper
Paprika
1 pound fresh cooked shrimp
1 large onion
1 6-ounce can sliced or chopped
    mushrooms

8 ounces grated sharp Cheddar
    cheese
1 tablespoon flour
2 tablespoons butter or juice
    from mushrooms
White wine or sherry

Sprinkle fish liberally with salt, pepper, and paprika and set aside. Cut up shrimp. Sauté onion in butter and add mushrooms. Drain off juice and save. Mix mushrooms, onions, and shrimp. Set aside. Using a generous tablespoon of flour, 2 tablespoons butter or juice from mushrooms (make juice equal 1 cup by adding white wine or sherry), make a thick white sauce. Place a large scoop of the shrimp, onion, and mushroom mixture in the middle of the fish, getting as much as possible inside the fish. Place in baking dish. Pour sauce over fish and top with grated cheese. Bake at 325 degrees for 1 hour. Sprinkle top with paprika and serve. Serve with baked halved tomatoes seasoned liberally with butter, basil, salt, and pepper, and garnished with parsley.

Yield: 8 servings
Nellie Dean

LOBSTER STURDEVANT

½ cup mayonnaise
⅓ cup catsup
1½ tablespoons snipped chives
1 teaspoon paprika

½ cup lemon juice
1 jigger brandy
1 pound lobster (crabmeat may
    be substituted)

Mix all ingredients well. Serve cold in ramekins or shells or on lettuce.

Yield: 4 to 6 servings
Dolly Moore

MARY SPENCER'S BAKED HADDOCK

1½ pounds haddock, or other
   flaky white fish
2 tablespoons lemon juice
1 teaspoon prepared mustard
   (Dijon preferred)

1 teaspoon Worcestershire sauce
½ teaspoon salt
Dash black or white pepper
1 small onion
1 cup milk (may be skim milk)

Wipe fish with a damp cloth. Place in 2 quart baking dish. Mix seasonings and spread over fish. Slice onion on top and pour milk over all. Bake about 25 to 30 minutes at 375 degrees. Garnish with parsley and lemon slices and serve with its own sauce poured over.

Yield: 6 servings
275 calories per serving
Sara Kidd

STUFFED ROCKFISH

8 ounces rockfish fillet
3 ounces crabmeat
1½ ounces Swiss cheese (grated)
1½ ounces Cheddar cheese
   (grated)
1 ounce mayonnaise
1 tablespoon Old Bay
   seafood seasoning

1 tablespoon mustard—dry
1 egg
2 ounces white wine
2 ounces butter
2 ounces mayonnaise
2 egg whites

Combine crabmeat, cheese, mayonnaise, egg, Old Bay, dry mustard, and mix well. Place white wine and butter in sauce pan, top with fish, skin down, place topping on fillet. Whip together 2 ounces mayonnaise and egg whites, pour over stuffed fish. Bake at 350 degrees 25 to 35 minutes, until topping is brown and has risen.

Yield: 2 servings
The Chambers
Chef Greg Wheatley
Easton, Md.

OYSTER PIE

4 medium potatoes	1½ teaspoons flour
1 pint oysters	2 tablespoons butter
2 stalks celery	2 cups medium white sauce
1 small onion	3 hard-cooked eggs, chopped
Salt and pepper to taste	Pie crust for one pie shell

Slice the potatoes and place one-half in bottom of 2-quart casserole. Simmer oysters and liquor until edges curl.

Sauté celery and onions in butter. Add flour, salt, and pepper. Place over potatoes. Add oysters, cover with rest of potatoes and add white sauce. Dot with 1 tablespoon butter. Mix in chopped hard-cooked eggs. Place in deep pie dish and cover with pastry. Bake at 450 degrees for 10 minutes. Reduce heat to 350 degrees. Bake for 45 minutes.

Yield: 6 servings
Carol Stockley

SCALLOPED CORN AND OYSTERS

1 quart oysters	1 teaspoon salt
2 cans (1 pound, 4 ounces) cream	Dash of Tabasco sauce
style corn	4 cups coarsely crumbled saltine
½ cup light cream	crackers
½ teaspoon pepper	1 cup melted butter

Mix cracker crumbs with melted butter and arrange layer of crumbs in bottom of 2-quart casserole. Drain oysters and chop coarsely. Mix corn with light cream and seasonings. Add a layer of corn mixture and a layer of oysters to casserole. Repeat layers, reserving enough crumbs to top casserole. Bake at 375 degrees for 40 minutes.

Yield: 10 servings
Dolly Moore

SCALLOPED OYSTERS

1 quart oysters (drained—reserve
   liquor)
1 teaspoon salt
2 tablespoons minced onion
2 tablespoons flour

⅛ teaspoon pepper
1 teaspoon Worcestershire sauce
½ cup butter
¾ cup milk
1½ cups crumbled crackers

Mix salt, pepper, onion, and flour into paste with liquor. Heat milk, slowly add paste to milk and stir until smooth. Remove from heat, add oysters and Worcestershire sauce, place in very shallow pan, sprinkle with crumbs and butter. Bake in 400 degree oven until brown (about 20 minutes). Serve hot. Great as buffet side dish.

Yield: 6 to 8 servings
Rita Rogers Kearney

TILGHMAN OYSTER PIE

1 pint oysters
1 medium or 2 small potatoes,
   diced
1 stalk celery, chopped

1 carrot, sliced
Salt and pepper to taste
2 tablespoons butter
1 recipe pastry—2 crusts

Drain oysters, save juice. Boil potatoes, carrots, and celery until almost fork tender. Drain. Prepare pastry. Line 9-inch pie pan with part of pastry. Alternate layers of vegetables and oysters. Salt and pepper each layer, dot with butter. Pour oyster juice over filling. Add top crust. Slit top. Bake at 450 degrees for 10 minutes. Reduce to 375 degrees for 30 to 35 minutes.

Yield: 4 small servings
Meriel Lord
Tilghman's Island, Md.

OYSTERS A LA GINO

2 tablespoons butter
⅓ cup all-purpose flour
1 tablespoon paprika
½ teaspoon monosodium
    glutamate
½ teaspoon garlic powder
½ teaspoon Chesapeake Bay-
    style seafood seasoning (if
    not available, add cayenne to
    other seafood seasoning)

½ teaspoon white pepper
1 cup milk
2 tablespoons Worcestershire
    sauce
2 tablespoons dry sherry
6 to 8 ounces cooked lump
    crabmeat (about 1 cup)
24 oysters on the half shell
6 slices bacon, cut into 4 pieces

Melt butter in a heavy pan over low heat; mix in flour and dry seasonings. Stir in the milk and Worcestershire sauce; whisk until smooth.
Cook until thickened, about 5 minutes, stirring constantly. Remove
from heat and add sherry. Cool mixture for 20 minutes. Gently mix in
crabmeat. Arrange oysters on a shallow baking pan; top each with a
tablespoon of crab mixture. Place a piece of bacon atop each. Bake in a
375 degree oven for 10 to 12 minutes or until bacon is crisp.

Yield: 6 to 8 servings
Robert Morris Inn
Oxford, Maryland

BAKED ROCK WITH POTATOES

1 3-pound rockfish
Salt
Pepper

4 potatoes (medium)
1 onion (large)
¼ cup butter

Salt and pepper the rock for baking. Slice potatoes and onion and put
around the rockfish, with butter. Put in about 1 inch of water and bake
about 1½ hours in 350 degree oven.

Yield: 4 servings
Caroline M. Allaband

BEST SCALLOPED OYSTERS

Serves 4
1 pint oysters
1 cup medium coarse saltine
   crumbs
½ cup melted butter
¾ cup light cream
¼ cup oyster liquid
¼ teaspoon Worcestershire sauce
½ teaspoon salt

Serves 28
1 gallon oysters
6 cups cracker crumbs
1 pound melted butter
6 cups cream
2 cups oyster liquid
2 teaspoons Worcestershire sauce
4 teaspoons salt

Drain oysters, reserving liquid. Combine butter and crumbs. Spread ⅓ of crumb mixture in shallow baking dish. Put half of oysters on crumbs, sprinkle with pepper. Use another ⅓ of crumbs, remaining oysters on top, sprinkle with pepper. Combine liquid ingredients and salt. Pour over oysters. Top with remaining crumbs. Bake in 350 degree oven for 40 minutes.

Yield: 4 or 28 servings
Kay Everngam

TILGHMAN ISLAND OYSTER FRITTERS

1 pint oysters, drained
1 cup flour
1 cup pancake flour
¾ teaspoon baking powder

1 egg
Salt and pepper to taste
¾ to 1 cup milk

Beat egg, add pancake flour, regular flour, baking powder, salt, pepper, and milk. Stir well. If needed, add a little more milk. Add oysters. Fry until golden brown by dropping mixture by tablespoons onto hot griddle containing 1 inch of grease.

Yield: 4 servings
"Rainy"

ESCALLOPED OYSTERS

1 quart oysters
3 cups crushed saltines
2 tablespoons butter
1 teaspoon chicken bouillon
    (granulated type)

Salt
Pepper

Mix crushed saltines with salt, pepper, and chicken bouillon. In a casserole, alternately layer cracker mixture and oysters, making last layer of cracker mix. Melt butter and add with enough milk to cover. Sprinkle with parsley and paprika. Bake at 325 degrees for 35 minutes.

Yield: 4 to 6 servings
Tidewater Inn
Easton, Md.

This young man, complete with rifle and Rough Rider hat, was the subject of a photographic Christmas card in the early 1900's.

GAME

SQUIRREL POT PIE

2 squirrels
1 large onion, chopped
3 medium potatoes, chopped
1 cup chopped celery
½ cup chopped carrots

1 teaspoon salt
⅛ teaspoon pepper
2 tablespoons flour
Pastry for 2 crust pie

Clean squirrels thoroughly and soak in salt water for at least 2 hours. Cover with water and simmer until meat is tender. Remove meat and skim broth. Add raw vegetables to broth. When vegetables are tender, thicken broth with 2 tablespoons flour, mixed with 4 tablespoons water. When smooth, add seasonings, squirrel meat and taste and adjust seasoning. Squirrel may be boned or left in pieces as desired. Line a glass or deep ceramic pie dish with pastry. Place squirrel, vegetables, and gravy in pastry and cover with top pastry. Crimp edges and cut vents in any design you prefer. Place pie in 425 degree oven and after 5 minutes, reduce heat to 350 degrees. Bake 20 to 25 minutes more until pastry is brown.

Yield: 5 to 6 servings
Elizabeth Ecker

MARYLAND FRIED QUAIL

8 quail with giblets
¼ cup flour
1 teaspoon salt
¼ teaspoon pepper

¼ teaspoon poultry seasoning
¾ cup shortening
¾ cup milk
¾ cup water

Clean quail and soak in salt water to release most of the blood. Pat dry and separate breasts and legs. Shake in a paper bag with flour and seasonings. Reserve left-over flour. Fry in hot shortening until tender. Remove legs first. Do not overcook. Remove all quail from drippings and add giblets. Brown giblets and shake in left over seasoned flour. You may need to add another tablespoon of flour. Brown flour, stirring vigorously. Add milk and water mixed, stirring until thickened. Serve the gravy over hot biscuits, along side the quail.

Yield: 4 servings
Mr. & Mrs. John W. Asher, Jr.

BRUNSWICK STEW

4 grey squirrels or
1 6-pound stewing chicken
2 large onions, sliced
4 cups fresh tomatoes, or
    2 1-pound cans
2 cups lima beans
3 medium potatoes, diced

4 cups fresh corn, or 2 1-pound
    cans
3 teaspoons salt
1 tablespoon sugar
½ teaspoon pepper
½ cup dry, white wine

Cut squirrel or chicken in pieces and simmer in 2 to 3 quarts water, enough to cover, until meat is tender, about 1½ hours for squirrel and 2¼ hours for chicken. Remove meat from bones. Add remaining ingredients to broth (not meat) and simmer uncovered until vegetables are tender. Add meat and serve. Better if made a day ahead and reheated.

Yield: 8 to 10 servings
Everett Adams

CHOPTANK FROG LEGS

6 pairs frog legs
2 eggs
Bread crumbs

1 lemon
Cooking oil

Thaw frog legs in ice and water. This insures moistness in the cooked legs. (This works well with fowl also). Cut pairs of legs into single legs with poultry shears or a sharp knife.

Put oil in frying pan (about ¼-inch deep) and heat to around 250 degrees. Beat eggs together in a shallow dish. Roll legs in egg and then in bread crumbs, covering completely. Put legs in hot oil and cook slowly turning as necessary (cooking too fast will dry out small part of leg and leave large part partially cooked). When bread crumbs are brown and legs are done, remove from pan and place on paper towels to drain. Squeeze juice from lemon over legs, season with salt and pepper if desired.

Yield: 2 servings
Bill Croll

MUSKRAT STEW

1 dressed muskrat per person	2 tablespoons flour per muskrat
½ cup cooking oil	¼ teaspoon salt per muskrat
1 large onion per muskrat	Dash of black pepper

Use only young, tender, muskrats, sometimes called Marsh Rabbit on the Eastern Shore. Cut up muskrats. Trim off any fat very carefully. Split back and separate ham half from shoulder half to make four pieces. Soak in salt water for four hours. Remove from salt water and drain well.

Mix flour, salt, and pepper in a paper bag. Shake muskrat pieces in bag until well coated.

Heat oil in heavy skillet. Sear meat in hot oil until meat is browned. Slice onion over meat until meat is deeply covered with onion slices. Place lid on pot and simmer until meat is very tender. Add water if needed.

OPTIONAL: one quartered potato for each muskrat may be added during the last 30 minutes of cooking if desired.

Yield: One muskrat per person
Dr. Howard F. Kinnamon

If a snapping turtle bites you, it will hang on 'til the sun goes down.

JUGGED HARE

1 2½-3 pound rabbit
4 tablespoons flour
1 teaspoon salt
⅛ teaspoon white pepper
6 slices bacon
2 oranges
½ cup chopped onion

⅛ teaspoon dried thyme
⅛ teaspoon dried marjoram
¼ teaspoon freshly grated
    nutmeg
1 cup water
1 cup dry sherry

Clean rabbit and cut into serving size pieces. Mix flour, salt, and pepper, and coat rabbit pieces. Melt butter and brown rabbit pieces slowly in a heavy skillet.

Line a bean pot with bacon slices and arrange rabbit pieces in pot. Add the chopped onion. Deglaze skillet with 1 cup water and pour over rabbit in pot. Grate orange rind and extract the juice. Add orange juice, orange rind, nutmeg, thyme, marjoram, and sherry to pot. Cover and bake slowly at 275 degrees for three hours, or until rabbit forks tender.

Yield: 4 to 6 servings
Sara Kidd

DIAMOND BACK TERRAPIN STEW

4 diamond back terrapin, from
    5 to 7 inches
½ livers from 4 terrapin
3 cups cooking liquor from
    terrapin
6 hard cooked eggs

¼ pound butter
½ teaspoon ground mustard
¼ teaspoon red pepper
Pinch of cayenne pepper
3 tablespoons lemon juice
½ cup Madeira wine

Terrapin must be live and active. Plunge them into a tub of cold water. This will activate them and cause them to clean themselves.

Then plunge the terrapin into boiling water to cover. Boil gently for at least one hour. When the feet hang limp in the water, they are done.

Remove shell and then find the liver. Locate the gall which looks like a black jelly bean. Remove gall with a sharp knife and do not break it, as it can ruin the meat. Remove the meat from the shell and discard gall, intestines, shell, and half of liver. Cut up terrapin meat.

Hard-cook the eggs. Remove shell and mash egg yolks. Reserve whites. Mash ½ of the livers from the four terrapin. Melt ¼ pound of butter and pour over livers. Mix with mashed egg yolks and cook with 3 cups of the liquor from cooking the terrapin. Add the mustard, red pepper, cayenne, and lemon juice. Add cut-up meat from the terrapin. Simmer and serve very hot. Add chopped egg whites. Pass Madeira wine to add to stew, as desired.

Note: In the early days of our history terrapin could be taken at any time and the terrapin eggs were highly prized to add to the stew. It is now illegal to use terrapin eggs or to take terrapin from April 1 to October 31. Chicken eggs are used as a substitute. Terrapin meat can be frozen.

Yield: 4 servings
Doug and Virginia Turnbull

DIAMOND BACK TERRAPIN STEW

2 terrapin at least 7 inches
    lengthwise of under shell
1 stalk of celery
1 carrot
1 medium onion
1 teaspoon pickling spices

Salt
Pepper
Cornstarch
Butter
Dry sherry

Remove heads from terrapin and soak in cold salt water over night. Scrub terrapin thoroughly and place in 4 to 6-quart pot. Coarsely chop celery, onion, and carrot and add to pot with seasonings and enough water to cover. Bring to a boil and simmer with a lid on for 1 to 1½ hours or until meat separates easily from the bones. Remove terrapin from water and pick off meat, discarding entrails, but saving eggs, liver, and heart. Remove gall sac from the liver with great care—do not allow gall sac to burst, and discard. Chop meat. Strain broth through a fine strainer. Thicken broth with cornstarch and add butter to taste. Add terrapin meat and eggs and a little dry sherry to taste. Serve over Maryland beaten biscuits.

Yield: 4 servings
Tidewater Inn
Easton, Md.

STEWED TEAL OR WOOD DUCK
AND SLIPPERY DUMPLINGS

2 ducks (each split in half)
1 can chicken broth

1 medium onion sliced
Salt and pepper

Combine all. Bring to a boil, cover and simmer 1½ hours or until ducks are tender.

Note: Turnips may be added to pot and cooked for last 20 minutes or so.

SLIPPERY DUMPLINGS

2 cups flour
1 teaspoon salt

½ cup (approximately) broth
  from pot

Note: Broth should be cooled before adding to flour.

Combine flour and salt in large bowl. Gradually stir in cooled broth until mix forms into ball. Roll out dumplings as thin as possible. Cut into 1x3-inch strips. Remove ducks (and turnips if used) from pot and bring to rapid boil. Add dumplings—stirring as you add them. Cook, uncovered, until tender.

Yield: Serves 2 or 3
L. T. Short

SNAPPER SOUP
(also known as TURTLE SOUP)

1 6-pound snapping turtle
3 medium onions
3 medium potatoes
½ cup butter
½ cup flour
½ cup water
1 cup sherry

1 teaspoon sugar
3 bay leaves
3 quarts water
1 teaspoon salt
½ teaspoon pepper
2 hard cooked eggs, chopped
2 tablespoons lemon juice

If possible, remove head from snapping turtle. Plunge turtle into boiling water in a large pail or lard can and scald thoroughly. Remove shell and clean out entrails. Separate legs and other sections and wipe off scales from legs and neck. Wash meat in warm, salted water and cut meat into small pieces. Cut onions and potatoes into small dice and cover with 3 quarts water in large pot. Add sugar, salt, bay leaves and pepper. Brown turtle meat in butter in large skillet until lightly brown. Remove meat and add to vegetables in pot. Blend flour into remaining butter in skillet and add ½ cup water. Add this roux to the pot and simmer slowly until vegetables and meat are tender. Add sherry and lemon juice and chopped hard cooked eggs. Stir until heated through. Remove bay leaves and serve very hot. Pass more sherry to float on top if desired.

Yield: 12 to 16 servings
Max Chambers

Note: The Chesapeake snapping turtle is a MEAN CRITTER—be careful of your fingers!!

BAKED VENISON STEAK

2 or 3 pounds venison steak
¼ cup flour
1 teaspoon salt or 2
    teaspoons garlic salt

½ teaspoon pepper
4 tablespoons bacon fat
1 cup burgundy wine

Cut steaks one-half inch thick. Dredge with flour, salt, and pepper, mixed. Brown on both sides in bacon fat. Transfer steaks to rack in baking pan. Pour burgundy wine over meat and baste occasionally while baking at 350 degrees for about one hour, or until steak is tender.

Yield: 6 to 8 servings
Mr. and Mrs. John W. Asher, Jr.

VENISON STROGANOFF

2 pounds venison
¼ cup flour
1 teaspoon salt
½ teaspoon pepper
½ cup chopped onion
4 tablespoons butter or oil

2 beef bouillon cubes
2 cups water
¼ cup chopped parsley
½ pound mushrooms, sliced
1½ cups sour cream
½ cup sherry

Cut venison into small chunks. Shake in paper bag with flour, salt, and pepper. Brown on all sides in hot butter or oil. Remove meat to pan or tray. Sauté onion in drippings and add bouillon cubes dissolved in water. Simmer gently for 5 minutes. Add parsley and mushrooms and return browned meat to the mixture. Simmer for only a few minutes, as overcooking toughens the meat. When meat is tender, reduce heat to warm and add the sour cream and sherry. Serve hot over rice, wild rice, or noodles.

Yield: 10 to 12 servings
Mr. and Mrs. John W. Asher, Jr.

WILD DUCK

2 ducks
1 medium potato, peeled, and
    quartered
1 medium onion, peeled, and
    quartered
1 medium apple, peeled, and
    quartered
3 slices bacon

Clean ducks and rinse with cold water. Put two of the potato, onion, and apple quarters in each body cavity. Cover ducks with water and lay the bacon slices across the top of ducks. Boil gently until tender.

Yield: 4 servings
Louetta Shaffer

WILD GOOSE

2 lemon halves
Salt
Pepper
Ginger
Mustard
Garlic powder
½ onion
3 slices salt pork
1 apple quartered
½ onion
1 cup red wine
3 cups orange juice
Flour
1 wild goose

Rub wild goose, inside and out with 2 lemon halves. Place remains inside goose cavity. Season with salt, pepper, ginger, mustard, and garlic powder. Line pan with aluminum foil. Place goose breast side up in pan. Dust with flour and place on top of goose slices from ½ onion and 3 slices salt pork. Place in goose cavity ½ onion, quartered, and 1 apple, quartered, also 1 cup of red wine. Pour over all 3 cups of orange juice. Cover securely with aluminum foil and cook at 400 degrees approximately 3 hours or until done (check at 2 hours). When cool, slice and serve with orange sauce, made from essence. If essence has evaporated, add more orange juice. Usually flour dusted over goose in beginning will make sauce thick enough. Baking time of goose depends on kind of goose, whether young and tender, or old and tough.

Yield: 4 servings
Louis L. Goldstein
Comptroller of the Treasury
Annapolis, Md.

GOOSE SANDWICH SPREAD

If you find yourself with what appears to be an old tough Canada goose or snow goose, use it this way.

1 goose	½ teaspoon pepper
Water enough to ½ cover goose	1 teaspoon oregano
1 cup wine vinegar	1 large onion
¼ cup salad oil	1 stalk celery
1 teaspoon ginger	1 teaspoon poultry seasoning
2 bay leaves	½ cup sweet pickle relish
1 tablespoon salt	¾ cup mayonnaise

Marinate the goose over night in the next eight ingredients, turning goose occasionally. Put the goose and marinade in a large pot. Add enough water to cover goose. Add onion, celery, and seasonings. Cover and boil until tender. Remove meat from carcass, discarding most of skin. Put meat through the fine blade of a meat grinder, or food processor. Mix meat well with pickle relish and mayonnaise and serve with crackers, or use in sandwiches. If the goose is large, you may need to increase pickle relish and mayonnaise.

Mr. and Mrs. John W. Asher, Jr.
(in memory of Howard Eley, who developed the recipe)

DRESSING

6 cups lightly toasted bread crumbs	¼ cup chopped celery
1 tablespoon butter	1 teaspoon salt
¼ cup chopped onion	½ teaspoon pepper
	½ teaspoon poultry seasoning

Sauté onion and celery lightly in butter. Add a little broth from ducks (½ cup), seasonings, and bread crumbs. Toss lightly. Place ducks in roasting pan or casserole and cover with dressing. Bake at 450 degrees until dressing is nicely browned.

Yield: 4 servings
Louetta Shaffer

BROILED GOOSE BREAST

1 "reasonably tender" goose	1 teaspoon salt
1 quart water	1 tablespoon oil
½ cup wine vinegar	1 teaspoon powdered ginger
½ teaspoon pepper	1 stick butter, melted
½ teaspoon garlic salt	¼ cup lemon juice
1 bay leaf	½ teaspoon poultry seasoning

Remove each side of the breast in a whole piece. Marinate the breasts in the next eight ingredients overnight, turning once or twice. Drain and broil slowly over charcoal, basting frequently with the butter, lemon juice and poultry seasoning, mixed. Do *not* overcook.

Slice the breasts diagonally, as the grain of a goose breast is different than that of any other fowl.

Yield: 6 servings
Mr. and Mrs. John W. Asher, Jr.

APPLE GOOSE

1 wild Goose	2 cups applesauce
2 apples	2 cups cider (or apple juice)

Apple Goose is best done on a charcoal or gas grill which has a lid. Fashion a foil pan with 3 to 4 inch sides a little larger than the goose. Place under the grill where the charcoal goes. This will catch the drippings from the goose and boil it off again keeping the bird moist. Pile the charcoal outside the pan. Do not be stingy. Light the fire.

While waiting for the charcoal to get white hot, prepare the goose. Make sure all the inedible parts have been removed from the cavity and the oil sacs on the tail are completely cut off. Quarter the apples and soak in the cider. When the fire is ready, stuff the apples in the cavity of the goose and place it on the grill breast side up over the foil pan. Pour the cider into the cavity until it runs out. Pour rest in foil pan. Smear applesauce on breast and legs. Cover and cook for 1½ to 2 hours depending on size of goose. (A meat thermometer will help). When done, remove and let cool before slicing.

Yield: 4 to 6 servings
Bill Croll

Along with seafood and wild game, chicken has long been a favorite main dish on Maryland tables. The family flock was important in colonial times.

MAIN DISHES

BEEF BOURGUIGNON

2 tablespoons shortening
5 medium onions, sliced
½ pound mushrooms, washed, trimmed and sliced
2 pounds boneless beef chuck or round steak cut into 1 inch cubes
¾ cup beef broth, canned may be used

1 teaspoon salt
¼ teaspoon marjoram leaves
¼ teaspoon thyme leaves
⅛ teaspoon pepper
1½ tablespoons flour
1½ cups burgundy wine

Melt shortening in large skillet. Add onions and mushrooms; cook and stir until onions are tender. Remove mushrooms and onions from skillet and drain. Brown meat in same skillet, adding shortening if necessary. Remove pan from heat. Sprinkle next 4 ingredients (seasonings) over meat. Mix flour and broth; stir into skillet. Heat to boiling, stirring constantly. Boil and stir 1 minute. Then stir in wine. Cover. Simmer 1½ to 2 hours until meat is tender. Liquid should always just cover meat. If necessary, add more broth and wine—1 part broth to 2 parts wine. Gently stir in onions and mushrooms when meat is tender. Cook uncovered 5 minutes until heated through.

Yield: 6 servings
Mrs. Warren M. Howell

QUICK AND EASY SHERRIED BEEF

3 pounds lean stewing beef
¾ cup sherry (dry or semi-dry)

2 cans mushroom soup, undiluted
½ package dried onion soup mix

Do not brown meat. Mix all ingredients in a 3-quart casserole and bake covered at 350 degrees for 3 hours.

Yield: 10 servings
350 calories per serving
Virginia Guinn

CRUNCHY BEEF BAKE

7 ounce package macaroni (2
   cups uncooked)
1 pound ground beef
1 can cream of mushroom soup
1 can tomatoes, cut up

¾ cup shredded cheese
¼ cup green pepper, finely
   chopped
¾ teaspoon salt
1 cup French-fried onions

Prepare macaroni; drain. Brown beef; drain. Combine all ingredients except onions. Pour half into 2 quart casserole, lightly greased. Add ½ cup onions. Pour remaining mixture over onions, cover and bake 30 minutes in 350 degree oven. Top with remaining onions. Bake 5 minutes longer.

Yield: 6 servings
Gertrude Brown

BAR B.Q. BEEF

4 pounds roast beef (boneless)
1 large diced onion
½ cup diced celery
2 tablespoons butter
1 cup catsup
¾ cup water
2 tablespoons vinegar

2 tablespoons Worcestershire
   sauce
2 tablespoons brown sugar
1 teaspoon dry mustard
1 teaspoon salt
¼ teaspoon pepper
2 teaspoons lemon juice

Roast beef until tender and slice in serving pieces. Put in casserole. Brown onion and celery in butter and add the remaining ingredients. Simmer about 10 minutes and pour over beef. Let stand a few hours or overnight so sauce goes through meat. To serve heat in 325 degree oven for 45 minutes.

Yield: 12 servings
Hettie Russell

CONNECTICUT BEEF SUPPER

2 pounds beef cubes
2 large onions sliced
2 tablespoons oil
Salt
Pepper
2 4½-ounce cans sliced
   mushrooms

4 potatoes
¾ cup sour cream
¾ cup milk
1 can cream of mushroom soup
2 packages shredded Cheddar
   cheese
Bread crumbs

Brown in oil in skillet with salt, and pepper, the two pounds of beef cubes and onion slices. Add sliced mushrooms, plus juice, and simmer for two hours. Spread in large casserole. Slice the potatoes on top. Mix and pour over the sour cream, milk, salt and pepper, and the cream of mushroom soup. Bake for one hour at 350 degrees. Sprinkle with shredded Cheddar cheese and bread crumbs on top. Bake 20 minutes more.

Yield: 4 to 6 servings
Barbara Quinn

CHILI CON CARNE

1 pound hamburger
3 tablespoons fat
1 green pepper
1 onion
⅛ teaspoon cayenne
1 tablespoon chili powder
1 teaspoon salt

2½ cups tomatoes
1 teaspoon hot sauce (optional)
1 can tomato soup
½ teaspoon paprika
1 bay leaf
1 clove garlic
2½ cups kidney beans

Brown the hamburger, pepper, and onion in fat in skillet. Drain any fat when done. Add the other ingredients (except beans) and simmer over low heat about 15 minutes to one-half hour. Add kidney beans and simmer until beans are heated through.

Yield: 6 servings
Mrs. William Patchett

SWISS STEAK

1½ pounds beef-round, chuck, or
    rump
1 medium sized onion, sliced
3 tablespoons chopped green
    pepper
Flour

3 tablespoons fat
1 can tomato sauce (8-ounce)
1 cup water
1½ teaspoons salt
¼ teaspoon pepper
1 teaspoon Worcestershire sauce

Pour flour onto steak and pound it in with edge of plate. Cook onion and green pepper in fat until tender. Brown meat on both sides in fat. Add tomato sauce, water, salt, pepper, and Worcestershire sauce. Cover and simmer for 1 to 1½ hours, or until meat is tender.

Yield: 4 servings
Rita Rogers Kearney

SWISS STEAK

1 2 to 2½ pounds beef top
    round steak (about 1½ inch
    thick)
2 tablespoons flour
3 tablespoons salad oil

2 large onions, thinly sliced
1 16-ounce can whole tomatoes
1 garlic clove, minced
1 teaspoon salt
Hot cooked noodles

About 3½ hours before serving, on cutting board, coat meat with flour; with edge of plate pound both sides of meat well. In 12-inch skillet over medium high heat, in hot salad oil cook meat until brown on both sides. Add onions and remaining ingredients except noodles. Heat to boiling, reduce heat to low, cover, simmer 3 hours or until meat is tender, turning once. Arrange meat and noodles on warm large platter. Serve sauce over them or pass sauce in gravy boat.

Yield: 8 servings
Margaret Blair

REUBEN BAKE

2 (27-ounce cans) sauerkraut
1 pound thinly sliced corned beef
2 cups shredded Swiss cheese
1 recipe rye biscuits
¼ cup butter
1 cup thousand island dressing

Drain sauerkraut, reserving 1½ cups liquid. Cut corned beef into bite size pieces. Combine kraut, 1½ cups liquid, dressing, corned beef and cheese in two 10x6x1¾-inch baking dishes. Bake at 350 degrees for 40 minutes. Increase oven to 425 degrees and top with rye biscuits. Brush with 2 tablespoons melted butter and bake 15 minutes more. This freezes well. The rye biscuits may be frozen in separate plastic bag, not on top of casserole. Rye biscuits should be baked 7 minutes at 425 degrees and cooled before freezing.

RYE BISCUITS

1½ cups sifted all purpose flour
6 teaspoons baking powder
1 teaspoon salt
1½ cups rye flour
1 teaspoon caraway seeds
½ cup shortening
1 cup plus 2 tablespoons milk

Sift white flour, salt, and baking powder, stir in rye flour, and caraway seed. Cut in shortening until mixture is coarse crumbs. Make a well in center and add milk all at once. Stir until dough clings together. Knead gently 10 to 12 times on lightly floured surface. Pat dough to ½ inch thick and cut out biscuits. Top your casserole or bake on greased baking sheet. Brush with butter. Bake at 425 degrees for 15 minutes.

Yield: 6 servings
Joyce Ziegler

KAREN'S CASSEROLE

1½ pounds ground beef
3 cups raw, sliced potatoes
2 large sliced onions
1 can (13-ounce) baked beans
1 can tomato soup

Place half of the ground beef in the bottom of a greased casserole dish, then a layer of half potatoes, next one half of the onions and beans. Repeat the procedure with remainder of ingredients. Season to taste. Top with can of tomato soup. Bake at 350 degrees for 1½ to 2 hours.

Yield: 8 servings
Karen Lee Brewington

MEAT BALLS

2 eggs
2 pounds ground beef
1 medium onion (chopped)
Salt (¾ to 1 teaspoon)

Pepper
1 8-ounce jar grape jelly
1 small bottle chili sauce
2 cups bread crumbs

Mix ground beef, onions, salt and pepper, bread crumbs, and eggs. Make into small balls. Add to sauce. Cook for one hour (low heat). Set over night. Scoop off fat on top, heat and serve.

Yield: 48-50 small balls
Barbara Quinn

EMPANADAS (Meat Pies)
Authentic Chile Recipe

Dough:
2 cups flour
2 tablespoons shortening
½ teaspoon salt

½ cup water
½ cup milk

Sift flour into bowl. Heat milk, add shortening, warm water, and salt. Pour this into flour and mix. Knead dough for about 10 minutes. Divide into 3 parts. Roll very thin. Fill with meat mixture or cheese. Fold over like a turnover. Seal edges. Fry in hot oil.

Meat Filling:
1 pound ground beef
1 pound onions
½ cup raisins
3 hard boiled eggs

1 teaspoon paprika
1 teaspoon cumin
Salt
Pepper to taste

Brown meat and onions, add ½ cup warm water, raisins, salt, pepper, paprika, and cumin. Cook for 10 minutes. Fill empanada dough with mixture and a slice of hard boiled egg.

For cheese empanadas, use mozzarella or muenster cheese. Put a piece of cheese in center of dough and seal very well with water so it does not open.

Yield: 6 to 8 servings
Carmen Howell

PASTEL DE CHOCLS
Authentic Chile Recipe

2 cans creamed corn
4 tablespoons butter
2 eggs
Salt

Pepper
Meat mixture (recipe of
    empanadas)
3 hard boiled eggs

Grease a pyrex baking dish. Put meat mixture in first. Slice 3 hard boiled eggs on top of meat. Beat the 2 egg yolks. Beat whites separately. Add yolks, salt, and pepper to taste to the corn and stir. Fold in whites. Spread this on top of meat and hard boiled eggs. Baste with butter and sprinkle with sugar. Bake at 400 degrees for 30 minutes or until light brown.

Yield: 4 to 6 servings
Carmen Howell

CARACAS

1 tablespoon butter
3 eggs
1 teaspoon chili powder
1 cup chipped beef (cut in strips
    or pieces)

1 pound grated cheese (mild
    Cheddar)
1 can tomatoes

Fry beef in pan with butter and chili powder until it curls. Have tomatoes hot and add to beef. Cook until tomatoes are tender. Add grated cheese and let it melt, then add slightly beaten eggs. Stir constantly and when done, season to taste with red and black pepper, salt and Worcestershire sauce. Serve on crackers, while hot.

Yield: 4 to 6 servings
R. Doris Stivers

MALAYA

1 flank steak
½ cup vinegar
Parsley
Salt and pepper
½ cup oil

2 hard boiled eggs
1 onion
2 carrots
Oregano

Marinate steak overnight in vinegar, salt, pepper, oregano, and parsley. Make a pocket in flank steak and fill with sliced carrots, chopped onion and sliced boiled egg. Roll it, tie it, or fasten with tooth picks. Brown meat in oil. Add 2 cups water and the marinade and cook for 20 minutes or until done. Serve with rice or potatoes. Can also be eaten cold with a salad.

Yield: 4 servings
Carmen B. Howell

SWISS STEAK

2 pounds round steak (pound in
    flour, salt, and pepper)
2 medium onions, chopped
2 cups canned tomatoes
1 teaspoon dry mustard

½ teaspoon chili powder
1 bay leaf
2 tablespoons Worcestershire
    sauce
2 tablespoons sugar

Fry steak in 2 tablespoons of fat. Add remaining ingredients. Simmer about 1 hour. It is better when re-heated.

Yield: 6 to 8 servings
Hettie Russell

PORCUPINE MEAT BALLS

1 pound ground beef
⅓ cup uncooked rice
¼ cup chopped onion
¼ cup water

Dash pepper
1 can condensed tomato soup
½ teaspoon chili powder
½ cup water

Combine meat, rice, onion, ¼ cup water, salt, and pepper. Shape into 15 one-inch balls. Blend soup and chili powder. Stir in ½ cup water. Bring to boil. Add meat balls, cover and simmer slowly 1 hour, stirring a few times.

Yield: 5 servings
Mildred James

CHILI

½ pound dried pinto beans
2 pounds coarse ground beef
1 pound coarse ground pork
¼ cup olive oil
3 large onions, chopped
1 quart water
6 tablespoons chili powder

4 teaspoons salt
5 cloves garlic, minced
1 teaspoon ground cumin
1 teaspoon red pepper
1 green pepper, chopped
1 tablespoon sugar
1 can tomato paste (small)

Cook beans until tender. Brown meat in oil with onion, garlic, and green pepper. Add water and rest of ingredients. Simmer slowly two to three hours. Add beans and simmer 1 more hour.

Yield: 4 quarts
R. Doris Stivers

Don't turn back home when you've forgotten something—you'll be sure to have bad luck!

STUFFED PEPPERS

6 large green peppers
1 pound ground beef
½ cup grated onion
3 tablespoons raw rice
1 egg, beaten
2 tablespoons cold water
2½ teaspoons salt

1 teaspoon black pepper
2 tablespoons vegetable oil
1 cup chopped onion
1 29-ounce can tomatoes, drained
3 tablespoons lemon juice
3 tablespoons sugar

Slice tops off peppers and remove seeds. Mix together meat, grated onion, rice, egg, water, 1½ teaspoons salt, ½ teaspoon pepper. Stuff peppers, replace tops. Heat oil in pan and sauté chopped onions 10 minutes. Mix tomatoes and remaining salt and pepper. Arrange peppers and pour tomatoes around. Cover and cook over low heat for 45 minutes. Add lemon juice and sugar. Cover and cook 30 minutes longer, or until peppers are tender. Baste frequently. Gravy should be sweet and sour.

Yield: 6 servings
Regina Mueller

EASY LASAGNE

1 pound ground beef
2 cloves garlic, minced
1 6-ounce can tomato paste
1 1-pound 4 ounce can tomatoes
   (2½ cups)
1 teaspoon salt
¾ teaspoon pepper

½ teaspoon oregano
1 package (8-ounce) lasagne
   noodles
1 8-ounce sliced Swiss cheese,
   cut up
12 ounces cottage cheese

Brown ground beef and garlic. Add tomato paste, tomatoes, salt, pepper, and oregano. Cover and simmer 20 minutes. Cook noodles as directed on package. Heat oven to 350 degrees. Alternate layers of meat sauce, noodles, and cheeses in baking dish, (11½x7½x1½-inch) beginning and ending with meat sauce. Bake 20 to 30 minutes.

Yield: 6 to 8 servings
Donna B. Kimball
Home Economics Extension Agent for
Caroline County

SPAGHETTI CASSEROLE

1 pound spaghetti	¼ teaspoon pepper
1 medium onion	1 can cream style corn
2 tablespoons oil	1 can tomato sauce
1½ pounds ground beef	2 cups grated cheese
1 teaspoon salt	

Cook spaghetti in salted water, drain. Sauté 1 medium onion in oil, add beef, salt, pepper, corn, tomato sauce, and grated cheese. Mix with spaghetti, put in casserole and add more grated cheese on top. Bake at 375 degrees until bubbly.

Yield: 6-8 servings
Mary Shawn Horsey

SPANISH NOODLES

2 slices bacon	1 teaspoon salt
½ cup chopped onion	4 ounces (3 cups) medium noodles
1 pound ground beef	¼ cup chili sauce
1 1-pound 12 ounce can tomatoes, cut up	½ cup chopped green pepper

In a large skillet cook bacon until crisp; remove from skillet. Drain on paper towel. Crumble and set aside. Add onion to bacon drippings in skillet; cook until tender, but not brown. Add meat, cook until browned. Stir in tomatoes, green pepper, chili sauce, salt, and dash of pepper. Add the uncooked noodles, cook, covered, over low heat for 30 minutes, or until noodles are tender, stirring frequently. Stir in bacon.

Yield: 4 servings
Regina Mueller

TEXAS HASH

2 large onions, sliced
2 green peppers, chopped
3 tablespoons vegetable
    shortening
1 pound ground beef

2 cups canned tomatoes
1 cup uncooked rice
1 teaspoon chili powder
1 teaspoon salt
¼ teaspoon pepper

Cook onions and green peppers slowly in shortening until onions are limp and golden. Add ground beef and sauté until the mixture falls apart. Add tomatoes, rice, and seasonings. Arrange in large casserole. Cover and bake at 375 degrees for 45 minutes.

Yield: 8 servings
Helen Thawley

TOMATO CHEESEBURGER PIE

1 pound lean ground hamburger
¾ cup chopped onion
4 eggs slightly beaten
½ cup milk
4 ounces shredded sharp cheese

1 teaspoon salt
½ teaspoon oregano
¼ teaspoon pepper
1 8-ounce can pizza sauce
6 triangles cheese

Prepare pie crust and fit in pan as for pastry. In a skillet brown beef and onions and drain. In mixing bowl combine eggs, milk, shredded cheese, salt, oregano, and pepper. Stir in meat mixture and turn in pie shell. Bake in oven set at 325 degrees for 35 or 40 minutes until knife comes out clean. Spread top with pizza sauce, bake 10 more minutes. Arrange cheese triangles on top in spoke-fashion, cut and serve as pie while still hot.

Yield: 6 servings
Mildred James

CHINESE MEATLOAF

1 pound ground beef
1 cup chopped onions
3 cups chopped celery
2 4-ounce cans mushrooms,
　drained
1 10-ounce can chicken rice soup

1 10-ounce can cream mushroom
　soup
2 cups chow mein noodles
½ cup cashew nuts, chopped
　(optional)

Brown meat, onions, and celery in frying pan. Pour in casserole and stir in other ingredients. Sprinkle few extra noodles over top for crunchiness and bake in 350 degree oven for 45 minutes. Serve with rice.

Yield: 4 to 6 servings
Betty Fleetwood

TOMATO MEAT SAUCE

½ cup olive oil
1 cup chopped onion
1 pound beef chuck (in one piece)
1 pound pork shoulder (in one
　piece)
14 cups (4 #2½ cans or 2 #3 cans)
　tomatoes
2 tablespoons salt

2 bay leaves
1¼ cups (4 6-ounce cans) tomato
　paste
4 large garlic cloves, minced
½ teaspoon black pepper
2 tablespoons oregano
2 tablespoons Worcestershire
　sauce

Heat oil in saucepan. Cook chopped onion in oil until soft. Add and brown beef and pork in oil. Sieve or purée tomatoes, add seasonings and pour over meat. Cover and simmer slowly for 2½ hours.

Mix together tomato paste, cloves, pepper, oregano, and Worcestershire sauce. Add to above mixure. Simmer uncovered slowly, stirring occasionally, for 2 hours or until thickened. If too thick, add 1 cup water.

Note: Meat from this sauce may be shredded and used for barbecue sandwiches (with barbecue sauce) or sloppy joes. Use this sauce, also, for spaghetti or other Italian dishes.

Yield: 5 quarts
Kay Everngam

SALAMI

10 pounds ground chuck
10 rounded teaspoons Tender Salt
(meat curing salt)
5 teaspoons mustard seed

5 teaspoons coarse ground pepper
5 teaspoons garlic salt
2 teaspoons hickory smoked salt
Peppercorns to taste

Mix all ingredients together thoroughly (knead with hands) and refrigerate. For the next three days mix (knead) once a day. On fifth day mix again and then make into rolls of approximately 1 pound each. Bake in oven on rack or broiler pan at 150 degrees for eight hours. Turn once every two hours (¼ turn). Cool and wrap and put in refrigerator. Will keep for at least two months in refrigerator.

Yield: 10 rolls
Barbara Maske

VEAL CUTLETS WITH MUSHROOMS

6 veal cutlets, each cut about
¼-inch thick
⅓ cup flour
Butter or margarine
1 garlic clove, halved

½ pound mushrooms, sliced
½ cup dry vermouth
¼ cup water
1 teaspoon salt
1 tablespoon chopped parsley

About 45 minutes before serving:
On cutting board with meat mallet pound veal cutlets lightly on both sides until about ⅛ inch thick. On waxed paper, coat cutlets lightly with flour. In 12-inch skillet over low heat, melt ¼ cup butter or margarine; add garlic and cook until garlic is golden; discard garlic, increase heat to medium-high; add 3 veal cutlets and cook until cutlets are lightly browned on both sides, turning once, with pancake turner remove veal cutlets to platter, keep warm. Repeat with remaining cutlets, adding more butter or margarine if necessary. Reduce heat to medium. To drippings in skillet add mushrooms, vermouth, water, and salt; cook, stirring until mushrooms are tender, about 5 minutes. Spoon mixture over meat; garnish with parsley.

Yield: 6 servings
Margaret Blair

MARYLAND KIDNEY STEW

1 pair veal kidneys
⅛ pound butter
1 chopped onion
3 tablespoons flour

2 quarts hot water
Salt
Pepper

Soak kidneys in cold salted water for an hour. Remove gristle and cut meat into small pieces. Place butter in skillet to melt, add onions and flour. Cook, stirring constantly, until golden brown. Add the water and cut up kidneys. Simmer from early morning until evening, allowing two hours to first come to a boil. On the following morning, again bring to a boil, season to taste, and serve over waffles or hotcakes. More water may be required on the first day of cooking if the gravy thickens too much. This is a favorite Sunday morning breakfast in Maryland.

Yield: 8 cups
Charles McC. Mathias, Jr.
United States Senator

VEAL PARMESAN

1½ to 2 pounds veal steak,
  (cutlets, rump, or shoulder)
  cut ¼ inch thick
1⅓ cups fine bread crumbs
⅓ cup Parmesan cheese
3 ounces mozzarella cheese

3 eggs
1 teaspoon salt
¾ teaspoon monosodium
  glutamate
¼ teaspoon pepper
⅓ cup olive oil

Pound veal cutlets thin. Mix bread crumbs and Parmesan cheese. Combine well beaten eggs, salt, monosodium glutamate and pepper.

Heat olive oil in skillet. Dip veal pieces in egg mixture, then in crumbs. Brown in olive oil on both sides and arrange in 11x7x1½-inch baking dish. Pour 2 cups tomato meat sauce over cutlets. Top cutlets (or pieces) with 3 ounces mozzarella cheese (6 slices). Bake at 350 degrees for 20 to 30 minutes until cheese is melted and slightly browned.

Yield: 6 servings
Kay Everngam

HAM AND PORK LOAF

2 pounds ground cured ham
1½ pounds ground pork
¼ teaspoon salt
Pinch of pepper

2 eggs, beaten
1 cup milk
1 cup rolled crackers

Mix well and shape into loaf. Place in lightly greased baking pan. Bake two hours at 350 degrees. Remove and pour sauce over loaf. Bake for 15 minutes, basting often.

SAUCE

1½ cups brown sugar
1 tablespoon mustard

½ cup vinegar
½ cup water

Boil until thickened.

Yield: 8 servings
Emily Pindell

SWEET AND SOUR PORK

1¼ pounds lean pork
2 tablespoons flour
1 teaspoon salt
2 tablespoons shortening
1 large green pepper, sliced
2 tablespoons sugar

1 tablespoon vinegar
1 tablespoon cornstarch
1 cup pineapple chunks
1½ cups water
1½ cups instant rice

Cut pork into one inch cubes, dredge with flour and salt and brown in hot shortening, turning often, for 20 minutes. Add green pepper and pineapple chunks. Combine sugar, water, vinegar, and cornstarch. Add to meat mixture and bring to boil. Add instant rice, cover and simmer for 5 minutes.

Yield: 6 to 8 servings
Dolly Moore

ORIENTAL HASH

2 tablespoons cooking oil
Dash garlic powder
1½ cups cubed cooked pork
2 cups shredded lettuce

2 cups cooked rice
3 tablespoons soy sauce
2 well beaten eggs

Heat oil in skillet, add garlic powder and pork, cook until meat is lightly browned. Add cooked rice and soy sauce. Cook 10 minutes, stirring occasionally. Mix in beaten eggs and cook 1 minute longer, stirring frequently. Remove from heat, add lettuce, and toss together.

Yield: 6 servings
Regina Mueller

PORK LOIN CENTERS

8 to 10 pounds pork loin center
    (bone in)
2 teaspoons salt
1 teaspoon pepper

2 tablespoons sage
1 quart sauerkraut
3 tablespoons brown sugar

Wipe meat with damp cloth. Salt and pepper meat and rub sage on the back of the bone.

Bake at 325 degrees for about four hours. Remove from oven and keep roast warm. To the meat juices, add sauerkraut and brown sugar. Simmer on top of stove for 20 to 30 minutes. Serve with sliced meat.

Yield: 12 to 15 servings
Prettymans Trading Center

PORK CHOPS L'ORANGE

2 oranges-peeled, sliced
4 1-inch thick pork chops
Salt
Pepper
Paprika

½ cup currant jelly
1 teaspoon dry mustard
⅛ teaspoon ginger
1 cup orange juice
¼ teaspoon Tabasco sauce

Season chops, brown on both sides. Mix remaining ingredients, pour over chops, cover and simmer 15 minutes. Uncover and cook 15 minutes longer. Top with orange slices, baste with pan juices, serve.

Chicken quarters also very good served this way.

Yield: 4 servings
Gary Brooks

ZUCCHINI-HAM-CHEESE PIE

1 large onion, thinly sliced
3 small zucchinis, chopped
1 large clove garlic, crushed
⅓ cup olive oil, or vegetable oil
2 cups cooked ham, slivered
1 cup (4 ounces) Swiss cheese,
    shredded
1 cup dairy sour cream

1 teaspoon dillweed
1 teaspoon salt
¼ teaspoon pepper
2 tablespoons melted margarine
½ cup bread crumbs
¼ cup grated Parmesan cheese
10-inch pie shell

Sauté first three ingredients in oil in large skillet for about 5 minutes. Remove from heat and add ham, Swiss cheese, sour cream, and seasonings. Mix until thoroughly combined. Spoon into 10-inch pie shell. Melt butter and stir in bread crumbs and Parmesan cheese with a fork. Sprinkle mixture in a 2-inch band around edge of pie, leaving center open. Bake at 350 degrees for 35 minutes. Let stand 10 minutes before serving.

Yield: 6 servings
Carolyn Serviss

SPARERIBS IN GARLIC VINEGAR

4 pounds country-style spareribs
1 cup cider vinegar
3 cups water
½ cup dry white wine
2 teaspoons crushed whole
coriander

2 teaspoons crushed whole cumin
5 to 6 cloves of garlic
¼ teaspoon cayenne
2 teaspoons salt

Make marinade of vinegar, water, wine, coriander, cumin, garlic, cayenne, and salt. Pour over spareribs and marinate, covered 4 days. Turn several times.

Remove meat, drain 30 minutes, arrange in single layer in roasting pan, add ½ cup water. Bake, uncovered, at 350 degrees for 2 hours. Cut between ribs to serve.

Yield: 4 servings
Patricia Brooks

BARBECUED SPARERIBS

4 pounds spareribs
2 tablespoons butter
½ cup chili sauce
2 tablespoons Worcestershire
sauce
2 teaspoons salt

1 cup chopped onions
⅓ cup vinegar
2 tablespoons horseradish
2 tablespoons steak sauce
½ teaspoon pepper

Cut ribs into pieces. Place ribs on cold broiler about 3 inches from flame and brown. Turn and brown other side. Put into roaster and cover with sauce. Bake in 350 degree oven for 1½ hours. Do not preheat oven.

To make sauce, sauté onions in shortening until brown, add remaining ingredients, and cook uncovered about five minutes. Stir often.

Yield: 4 servings
Barbara Maske

HAM AND BROCCOLI FAMILY SUPPER

½ to 1 cup herb seasoned
    stuffing
1 package frozen broccoli, cooked
    and drained
2 cups cooked sliced ham

1 can cream of chicken soup
1 soup can of milk
2 tablespoons margarine
Sliced Swiss cheese
Paprika

Arrange herb stuffing, broccoli, ham and mixture of soup and milk in layers in greased 6x9-inch baking dish. Dot with margarine. Lay slices of Swiss cheese across top, sprinkle with paprika. Cover. Bake at 350 degrees for 30 minutes.

Yield: 4 servings
Caroline Allaband

STUFFED HAM

1 corned or sweet-pickled ham
    (14 to 16 pounds)
6 pounds cabbage sprouts

2 pounds chopped onions
¼ ounce crushed red pepper
Salt as desired

With a large butcher knife, stab holes or pockets into the ham about 2 inches apart all the way over.

Chop cabbage and mix with onions and red pepper. Salt will depend on taste and saltiness of the ham. Salt is rarely needed. Stuff the holes in the ham with the cabbage mixture. Wrap the ham (now three times its size) in cheese-cloth or an old pillow slip. Place in a large pot, and completely cover with cold water. Boil steadily for twenty minutes per pound. Allow to remain in water until water and ham are cool. Then remove ham from water and place in refrigerator, and allow to chill 12 hours before slicing.

In case no cabbage sprouts (the dark green shoots left in the spring after harvesting the cabbage in the fall—one of the few green vegetables available in the spring in colonial days) are available, cabbage may substitute. Also, since the invention of foil, the stuffed ham may be wrapped firmly in foil and baked at medium high temperature for thirty minutes per pound of ham. The cabbage and the baking give about the same results as the original recipe and the clean-up is much easier.

Yield: about 40 servings
Kathryn Curley

MOTHER DYSON'S RECIPE FOR
MARYLAND STUFFED HAM

12 pound corned ham or country
    cured ham
6 pounds cabbage
3 pounds onions
1 pound kale

2 tablespoons celery seed
Salt
Black pepper
Red pepper

Blanch kale, chop cabbage, and onions in small pieces (if you can stand the tears from the onions). Mix all together and add seasonings. (Never measured red pepper in my life—just sprinkled on mixture until hands begin to burn slightly while mixing. Some of my neighbors scald their mixture before packing into ham—guess I got too anxious to get the ham packed so I started packing as soon as I had it mixed.) To get ham ready for packing, cut deep slits in the ham, opposite from the way you slice the ham.

Pack and push as much stuffing mixture into holes as you can, covering top of ham if you have any left over. Put into clean cheese cloth bag. (I use a pillow case because its easier to just tie at top and not much chance of stuffing falling out.) Cook in large pot at least 4 hours and start timing when water begins to boil, and keep boiling entire time. Place a rack (I use an aluminum pie tin) in bottom of pan, to prevent ham from sticking to bottom. Cool before slicing.

Note: Juice from pot when ham is removed is excellent for seasoning vegetables.

Yield: Forty-eight 4-ounce servings
Roy Dyson, Congressman
1st Congressional District

Boil an egg and sprinkle it with pepper. Set a place at the table and put the egg there. Leave the door open, turn the light down low and at the stroke of midnight the wind will blow. The first man who comes in that door and eats the egg will be your husband.

BRUNSWICK STEW

1 hen
2 pounds veal
2 pounds pork
3 pounds white potatoes
1 pound onions

3 cans tomatoes
2 cans butter beans
1 can corn
1 red pod pepper
Salt

Cook all the meat together. When done, pull the meat apart. Heat tomatoes, onions and stock until onions are tender. Add butter beans and meat to mixture. When thoroughly heated, add the corn. This needs to be stirred constantly to keep it from sticking. Add seasoning last, enough to flavor.

Yield: 32 servings
Mrs. Ronald Bamford

SMITHFIELD HAM

1 10 to 12-pound ham

Soak ham in cold water overnight (if over 1 year old). If under a year, it does not need soaking. Scrub ham good. Preheat oven to 500 degrees. Place ham in a covered roaster with 6 cups cold water. Close all vents. Bake ham 30 minutes. Turn off oven. Allow ham to remain in oven without opening door for 3 hours. Turn heat to 500 degrees and leave 15 minutes. Turn off heat and allow to remain in oven for at least 3 hours. It can be left in oven overnight. Remove ham from roaster and cut off rind. May be served "as is", or it may be glazed.

Yield: 30 servings
Kay Everngam

"Mongst ye come" is the Eastern Shore way of saying, all of those among you come.

SWEET AND SOUR PORK

1 package pork gravy mix
1 cup pineapple juice
½ cup pineapple chunks

3 tablespoons vinegar
⅛ teaspoon ginger
3 cups cooked pork, cut in pieces

Combine all ingredients in 1 quart casserole and bake at 350 degrees for 40 minutes.

Yield: 6 servings
Virginia Brown

PORK CHOPS WITH LIMA BEANS

1½ cups dried lima beans
4 cups boiling, salted water
4 pork chops
2 sliced onions

1 can mushroom soup
½ cup milk
1 teaspoon caraway seeds

Soak beans as directed on package. Drain, cook in salted water 30 minutes. Drain. Brown chops. Place chops in bottom of baking pan. Add limas, top with sliced onions. Mix soup and milk, pour over all. Sprinkle seeds on top. Bake at 375 degrees for 1 hour, uncovered.

Yield: 4 servings
Beth Adams

AFRICAN CHOW MEIN

1 cup rice uncooked
1½ pounds pork, or veal, cubed
2 medium onions diced
2 cups celery chopped
2 cans chicken soup

2 cans mushroom soup
4 cans water
1 cup mushrooms
Salted almonds, if desired

Brown meat and onions; add remaining ingredients (uncooked). Bake 1 to 1¼ hours at 350 degrees.

Yield: 12 servings
Louise Schwartz

GARLIC SAUSAGE

1½ heads crushed garlic in
    1 cup of water
20 pounds ground fresh pork
    (fresh pork shoulders,
    skinned and boned, are
    recommended)

9 tablespoons salt
1 teaspoon allspice
1 tablespoon pepper
1 tablespoon paprika

Let garlic stand in water over night. Discard garlic, strain the water, and mix it and the rest of the ingredients thoroughly. You will have to use your hands.

Yield: 20 pounds
Regina Mueller

SAUSAGE STRING BEAN CASSEROLE

1 pound pork sausage
1 pound fresh string beans (or
    1 #2 can)
1 recipe medium white sauce

1 teaspoon salt
¼ teaspoon pepper
1 small onion, diced

Prepare sausage in patties. Fry in small amount of fat. Drain on paper towel. Cook string beans in small amount of water to which salt has been added. When tender, add diced onion. Place sausage patties in bottom of greased casserole, add string bean mixture; add white sauce. Bake in 350 degree oven for 20 minutes.

Note: Favorite cream soup may be substituted for white sauce. Topping of bacon bits, shredded cheese, or bread crumb topping adds to appearance.

Yield: 6 servings
Virginia Brown

SAUSAGE LOAF

1½ pounds bulk pork sausage
6 tablespoons cornmeal
¾ cup evaporated milk

1 10½-ounce can tomato soup
¼ cup water

Grease shallow baking pan. Mix thoroughly, or until milk is absorbed. Wet fingertips and shape mixture into oblong loaf 8x4x3-inch. Put into pan. Bake 15 minutes. Pour over and around, mixture of 10½-ounce can of tomato soup and water. Bake 1 hour in 350 degree oven. Baste.

Yield: 1 loaf
Virginia Brown

TOMATO SAUSAGE

1 pound ground pork
1⅓ tablespoons sausage
    seasoning

12 drops Tabasco sauce
4 tablespoons tomato paste

Mix thoroughly, refrigerate well before using. Then form into links or patties and fry. This does not keep for a long period of time. Use within a few days.

Yield: 1 pound
Hannah Adams

SAGE SAUSAGE

20 pounds ground fresh pork
7 tablespoons ground sage
½ cup sugar

9 tablespoons salt
1 tablespoon pepper

Fresh pork shoulders, skinned and boned, recommended. Blend all ingredients thoroughly. You will have to use your hands to do this.

Yield: 20 pounds
Regina Mueller

HERBED LEG OF LAMB

5½ to 6 pound leg of lamb
2 cloves garlic
1 tablespoon dry mustard
2 teaspoons salt

⅛ teaspoon pepper
½ teaspoon thyme
¼ teaspoon rosemary
1 tablespoon lemon juice

Rub lamb with 1 clove peeled garlic. Sliver remainder plus other clove of garlic. Slit lamb at intervals and insert garlic slivers. Blend mustard, salt, pepper, herbs, and lemon juice. Spread over entire surface of meat. Place on rack and bake, uncovered, at 325 degrees for 2 to 2½ hours. Thermometer should register 150 degrees (medium rare) or 160 degrees (medium well done) or 175 degrees (well done). Baste occasionally with pan drippings. Use pan juices to make a gravy, if desired.

Yield: 6 to 8 servings
Everett Adams

TUNA TETRAZZINI

½ package (4 ounce) spaghetti
2 6½-ounce cans chunk style tuna
½ cup chopped pimento
½ cup chopped green pepper
1 small onion, chopped

½ cup water
1 can cream of mushroom soup
1¾ cups grated sharp cheese
Salt and pepper

Break the spaghetti into small pieces and cook in salted water until tender. Drain. Put tuna, pimento, green pepper, and chopped onion in a casserole. Mix water and soup and add to tuna mixture. Add 1¼ cups cheese, the spaghetti and season to taste. Toss lightly until well mixed and coated with sauce. Sprinkle with remaining cheese. Bake in a moderate 325 degree oven about 45 minutes.

Yield: 8 servings
Mrs. Ronald Bamford

CHICKEN BREASTS SUPREME

4 chicken breasts—debone and
   skin
½ teaspoon lemon juice

¼ teaspoon salt
Big pinch white pepper
4 tablespoons butter

Preheat oven to 400 degrees. Rub breasts with drops of lemon juice and sprinkle lightly with salt and pepper. Heat butter in heavy, fireproof casserole (10-inch size) until it is foaming. Quickly roll the breasts in the butter, lay waxed buttered paper over them, cover casserole with lid and place in hot oven. After 6 minutes press top of breast with your finger. If still soft, return to oven for a moment or two. When the meat is springy to the touch, it is done. Remove meat to a warm platter and cover while making the sauce (2 to 3 minutes).

SAUCE

¼ cup white stock (chicken
   bouillon)
¼ cup dry white vermouth
1 cup whipping cream

Salt
Pepper
2 tablespoons fresh minced
   parsley (optional)

Pour bouillon and wine into the casserole with butter and boil down quickly over high heat until liquid is syrupy. Stir in the cream and boil down again over high heat until cream has thickened slightly. Turn off heat, taste carefully for seasoning, and add drops of lemon juice to taste. Pour the sauce over the meat, sprinkle with parsley and serve at once.

Note: Do not cook the chicken breasts too long as the meat will toughen, even a minute too much will make the meat dry. Serve with buttered asparagus tips, green peas, or spinach. Rice is excellent with the Breasts Supreme.

Yield: 4 servings
Edna Parrish

ALMOND CRUSTED CHICKEN BREASTS

4 boned chicken breasts	1 teaspoon paprika
1 cup sour cream	¾ teaspoon salt
1 teaspoon lemon juice	¼ teaspoon pepper
1 teaspoon Worcestershire sauce	1 cup bread crumbs
1 teaspoon celery salt	½ cup chopped almonds

Preheat oven to 375 degrees. Mix sour cream and seasonings. Dip chicken in mixture. Shake in bag of crumbs and nuts mixed together. Bake on greased pan 1 hour—uncovered.

Yield: 4 servings
Beth Adams

STIR-FRIED CHICKEN & MUSHROOMS

1 cup regular long grain rice	¼ teaspoon sugar
2 whole large chicken breasts	⅛ teaspoon garlic powder
2 tablespoons soy sauce	1 pound medium mushrooms
2 tablespoons cooking or dry sherry	4 green onions
2 teaspoons cornstarch	Salad oil
1 teaspoon minced gingerroot or ¼ teaspoon ground ginger	1 cup frozen peas, thawed

Thirty minutes before serving, prepare rice as label directs; keep warm. Meanwhile, cut each chicken breast lengthwise in half; remove skin and bones. Then with knife held in slanting position, almost parallel to the cutting surface, slice across width of each half into ⅛ inch thick slices. In medium bowl, mix chicken, soy sauce, sherry, cornstarch, gingerroot, sugar, and garlic powder; set aside. Thinly slice mushrooms; cut each green onion crosswise into 3 inch pieces. In 12 inch skillet or wok over medium-high heat, in ¼ cup hot salad oil, cook mushrooms and green onions, stirring quickly and frequently, until mushrooms are tender, about 2 minutes. With spoon, remove mushroom mixture to bowl. In same skillet or wok over high heat, in 3 more tablespoons hot salad oil, cook chicken mixture, stirring quickly and frequently, until chicken is tender, about 2 to 3 minutes. Return mushroom mixture to skillet; add peas, heat through. Serve with rice.

Yield: 4 servings
Barbara Quinn

CHICKEN & BROCCOLI CASSEROLE

2 10-ounce packages broccoli
(frozen)
4 whole chicken breasts
2 cans cream of chicken soup

1 cup mayonnaise
1 tablespoon lemon juice
1 cup Parmesan cheese
½ cup bread crumbs

Cook broccoli until tender; cook and debone chicken, cut into bite size pieces. Grease pan, and line with broccoli, put in chicken. Combine soup, mayonnaise, lemon juice, and pour over all—sprinkle with cheese and bread crumbs. Bake 30 minutes at 350 degrees.

Yield: 8 servings
Barbara Quinn

LOW CAL CHICKEN

¼ teaspoon orange zest
½ cup orange juice
1 tablespoon chopped green onion
1 teaspoon instant chicken
bouillon
3 medium chicken breasts,
skinned and split

1 tablespoon cornstarch
1 tablespoon cold water
3 orange slices, halved
½ cup seedless green grapes,
halved

Mix orange zest, orange juice, onion and bouillon. Coat chicken with mixture and place in a 9x13-inch baking dish. Cover with foil and bake at 350 degrees for 50 minutes. Pour off juices and add water to make ¾ cup. Add cornstarch mixed with 1 tablespoon water. Cook until thick. Sprinkle chicken lightly with salt, pepper, and paprika. Place half slice of orange on each piece of chicken and add grapes. Put under broiler until fruit is heated through.

Yield: 6 servings
Regina Mueller

POULET AU VIN

2 pounds chicken parts
¼ cup butter or margarine
1 10½-ounce can cream of
    mushroom soup

½ cup sherry (optional)
Dash pepper
10 small onions

Brown chicken in butter in large skillet. Stir in soup, sherry, and pepper, add onions, cover, simmer 45 minutes or until chicken is tender. Stir often. If desired, add ½ teaspoon whole thyme when browning chicken and substitute ⅓ cup water for sherry, omit pepper.

Yield: 4 to 6 servings
Grace Bamford

If you sing before breakfast, you'll cry before dark.

CHICKEN BROCCOLI BAKE

2 chicken breasts
2 tablespoons melted margarine
1 16-ounce package frozen
    broccoli
1 10¾-ounce can cream of
    mushroom soup undiluted

½ cup milk
½ cup shredded Cheddar cheese
¼ cup bread crumbs
Paprika

Place chicken in a 9-inch square pan and drizzle with melted margarine. Bake at 375 degrees for 40 minutes. Cook broccoli according to package and drain, arrange around chicken. Combine soup, milk, and cheese, pour over chicken and broccoli, sprinkle with bread crumbs and paprika. Bake an additional 20 minutes.

Yield: 4 servings
Mrs. Charles A. Rainey

WAISTLINE BARBECUED CHICKEN

2 tablespoons salad oil
4 whole chicken breasts (about 3
    pounds), split
3 cups tomato juice
½ cup vinegar
1 tablespoon granulated sugar
4 medium onions, sliced

3 tablespoons Worcestershire
    sauce
½ cup catsup
4 teaspoons prepared mustard
1 teaspoon pepper
2 teaspoons salt

Preheat oven to 350 degrees. In skillet, in oil, brown chicken well on all
sides. Remove to shallow baking pan. In saucepan, heat tomato juice
and remaining ingredients; pour over chicken. Bake, uncovered, 40
minutes, or until tender, basting every 10 minutes with sauce.

Yield: 8 servings
245 calories per serving
Sara Kidd

CHICKEN WITH HERBS

1 2½ to 3 pound fryer
½ cup salad oil
2 tablespoons minced parsley
½ teaspoon dried rosemary
½ teaspoon dried savory
2 tablespoons minced onion

1 peeled clove garlic, minced
1½ teaspoons salt
Speck pepper
3 tablespoons flour
1½ cups milk

Cut up chicken as for frying. Wipe each piece with clean, damp cloth. Arrange in shallow pan, then brush with salad oil. Bake in 500 degree oven
for 30 minutes, or until golden brown. Reduce temperature to 300
degrees and brush again with salad oil. Continue baking 15 minutes,
basting frequently. Then add parsley, rosemary, savory, onion, garlic, 1
teaspoon salt and pepper to rest of oil. Pour this mixture over chicken.
Bake until chicken is tender, about 15 minutes longer. Remove chicken
to hot platter; stir flour and remaining salt into fat left in baking pan.
Gradually add milk, while stirring. Cook over low heat, stirring constantly, until smooth and thickened. Pour gravy over chicken.

Yield: 4 servings
Mrs. Ronald Bamford

CHICKEN ST. JOHN

8 chicken breasts
½ pint sour cream
1 can of cream of chicken soup

1 package chipped beef
Paprika

Remove skin from chicken breasts. Wrap in chipped beef. Place in buttered baking dish. Heat together ½ pint sour cream and chicken soup. Pour mixture over chicken and sprinkle with paprika. Bake 4 hours in 200 degree oven.

Note: Delicious served with rice or poppy seed noodles.

Yield: 8 servings
Louise Schwartz

TURKEY OR CHICKEN DIVAN

2 10-ounce packages frozen
    broccoli or 1 bunch fresh
    broccoli
16 slices turkey or chicken breast
4 tablespoons butter
4 tablespoons flour
1½ cups milk
1 teaspoon salt
Dash of pepper

1 cup grated sharp Cheddar
    cheese
½ cup dry sherry
2 tablespoons lemon juice
½ teaspoon freshly grated
    nutmeg
¼ cup grated Parmesan cheese
½ cup slivered almonds

Butter a flat 2 quart casserole or baking dish. Arrange spears of cooked broccoli in dish. Leave broccoli slightly undercooked. Arrange slices of turkey or chicken on broccoli and pour the following sauce over it. Melt 4 tablespoons butter, blend in flour and milk. Simmer until thick and smooth. Add salt, pepper, and grated sharp cheese. Remove from heat and add sherry and lemon juice. Stir in nutmeg and Parmesan cheese. Pour sauce over casserole and sprinkle with almonds. Bake 20 minutes at 350 degrees or until heated through and bubbly. Almonds should brown slightly. Serve at once.

Yield: 8 servings
Marguerite Stanford

CHICKEN-CURRY FRITTERS

1 cup flour
1½ teaspoons baking powder
½ teaspoon salt
1 egg beaten
½ cup milk

½ cup cubed, cooked chicken
2 tablespoons chopped parsley
¼ cup grated onions
½ teaspoon curry powder

Sift flour, baking powder, and seasonings. Combine milk and egg. Add to flour. Fold in chicken, parsley, and onions.

Heat ½ cup oil about 3 minutes. Drop batter by tablespoon. Turn when brown. Drain before serving.

Yield: 12 fritters
Ruth Evans

CHICKEN, MIXED VEGETABLES, RICE DISH

1 envelope dried onion soup mix
½ cup uncooked rice
1 box (10-ounce) frozen mixed
   vegetables, broken apart
2 teaspoons chicken bouillon
   powder

3 cups water
8 pieces chicken (one 3 to 3½
   pound chicken)
Fresh ground pepper
Paprika

Reserve 2 tablespoons dried onion soup mix. Combine remainder of soup mix with mixed vegetables, and rice. Put mixture in greased 9x13-inch dish (one layer). Arrange chicken pieces on top of mixture. Bring to boil water, add chicken powder and mix well. Pour chicken bouillon broth over chicken (do not cover tops of chicken pieces) Sprinkle reserved onion soup mix, paprika, and ground fresh pepper over chicken pieces. Cover tightly with aluminum foil. Bake 30 minutes in 375 degree oven. Remove foil, baste chicken pieces, and bake additional 30 minutes until done.

Yield: 3 generous servings
Betty J. Brown

CHICKEN FRICASSEE WITH PARSLEY SAUCE

4 pounds chicken, cut in serving
   pieces
4 tablespoons oil
1 clove garlic, sliced

1½ teaspoons salt
Dash of pepper
1½ cups water

Heat oil and brown garlic in frying pan. Remove garlic, cook chicken in same oil until brown on all sides. Season with salt and pepper, add water and cook covered until tender. Serve with parsley sauce.

PARSLEY SAUCE

2 tablespoons butter
2 tablespoons flour
1 cup light cream
1 cup chicken stock (boil a
   back or rump)

½ cup parsley, chopped
½ teaspoon salt
Yolk of two eggs
1 teaspoon lemon juice

Melt butter and add flour, blend well, and add cream and stock slowly, stirring constantly until sauce is smooth and thickened. Add parsley and salt and bring to boil. Beat yolks and lemon with a little of the hot sauce and gradually stir into remaining sauce. Cook, stirring over low heat, for about 3 minutes, or until eggs are cooked. Pour over chicken on serving plate. Can be served with rice.

Yield: 6 servings
St. Michaels Harbour Marina, Inc.
St. Michaels, Maryland 21663

COQ AU VIN

6 boned and skinned chicken
    breasts—cut in half
Flour
Salt and pepper
1 can cream of chicken soup

1 can cream of mushroom soup
¾ cup sherry
Chicken drippings
Butter
½ pound mushrooms (sautéed)

Roll chicken breasts in seasoned flour, brown in butter and place in casserole, add ½ pound sautéed mushrooms. Combine chicken soup, mushroom soup, sherry, and chicken drippings. Pour over chicken and bake in covered casserole for 1¼ hours at 350 degrees. Serve over rice.

Yield: 12 servings
Hettie Russell

HOT CHICKEN SALAD

3 cups diced cooked chicken
1 cup finely chopped celery
2 teaspoons chopped onion
½ cup sliced almonds
1 10¾ ounce can cream of
    chicken soup (undiluted)
1½ cups cooked rice

1 tablespoon lemon juice
½ teaspoon salt
¼ teaspoon pepper
¾ cup mayonnaise
¼ cup water
2 cups crushed potato chips
¾ cup shredded Cheddar cheese

Combine first 9 ingredients—toss gently and set aside. Combine mayonnaise and water; beat with wire wisk until smooth. Pour over chicken mixture; stir well. Spoon into a greased 2 quart shallow baking dish; cover and refrigerate 8 hours or overnight. Bake at 450 degrees for 10 or 15 minutes until heated thoroughly. Sprinkle with potato chips and cheese; bake an additional 5 minutes.

Yield: 6 to 8 servings
Mary Jo Shaffer

CHICKEN AND RICE

1 chicken broiler-fryer cut up
1 can cream of chicken soup
1 can cream of mushroom soup
1 can cream of celery soup

1 can cheese soup
1 can water (soup can)
1 cup rice

Put in casserole and stir, salt chicken and lay on top of soup and rice mixture. Sprinkle with paprika. Bake 3 hours at 325 degrees covered with aluminum foil. Remove foil during last ½ hour.

Yield: 4 to 6 servings
Barbara Maske

CHICKEN MARANGO

1 3 to 3½ pound cut up fryer
Cooking oil
1 can tomato soup
1 can mushroom soup

½ cup mushrooms (optional)
½ cup chopped green peppers
   (optional)

Coat chicken with flour, salt, and pepper. Brown in skillet with ¼ inch cooking oil. When nicely browned, remove from pan. Reserve ¼ cup liquid for gravy. Make gravy, adding 1 can tomato soup, and 1 can mushroom soup. Add mushrooms and chopped pepper. Arrange chicken in oblong pan, cover with gravy, and bake for one hour at 350 degrees. Serve over cooked rice arranged on a platter.

Yield: 6 servings
Betty Serviss

When the Eastern Shoreman goes out to rake the pine needles, he says he is "raking up the pine shatts".

CHICKEN CORDON BLEU

6 thin slices ham
6 thin slices of Swiss cheese
6 split chicken breasts, boned
1 can cream of chicken or
    mushroom soup

1 can water
Paprika
½ cup corn flake crumbs
Salt
Pepper

Flatten chicken breast with mallet. Sprinkle with salt and pepper. Place a slice of ham and slice of cheese on each chicken breast and roll up. Hold in roll with 2 toothpicks. Place chicken rolls in a casserole dish. Dilute soup with equal parts water and pour over breasts. Sprinkle with corn flake crumbs and dash of paprika. Bake at 325 degrees for 1 hour.

Yield: 6 servings
Donna B. Kimball
Home Economics Extension Agent
for Caroline County

SWEET 'N SMOKEY CHICKEN

1 chicken, cut in serving pieces
1 large onion, sliced
2 teaspoons hickory smoked salt
¼ teaspoon pepper

½ cup catsup
¼ cup vinegar
½ cup maple syrup
2 tablespoons prepared mustard

Place onion slices in bottom of shallow baking pan Place chicken in single layer, skin side up, on top of onion. Sprinkle with hickory salt and pepper. Combine remaining ingredients and pour over chicken. Bake, uncovered, at 350 degrees for approximately one hour or until done.

Yield: 4 servings
Frank Perdue

WALTON'S CHICKEN SALAD

1 3 to 3½-pound chicken (2½
    to 3 cups cut up)
2½ to 3 cups chopped celery
2 chopped cucumbers
5 hard boiled eggs
1 tablespoon flour

1 teaspoon salt
1 teaspoon dry mustard
½ cup chicken broth
½ cup vinegar
2 tablespoons sugar
2 tablespoons butter

Cook chicken and chop. Add celery, cucumber, 2 hard cooked eggs, chopped, and whites of other 3 eggs. Mash 3 egg yolks, add flour, salt, pepper, mustard. Gradually add broth. Stir into this mixture vinegar, sugar, and butter. Cook until thickened. Cool and pour over salad mix.

Yield: 10 to 12 servings
Walton Johnson, III

BAKED CABBAGE CASSEROLE

1 head of cabbage
2 eggs
1 cup milk
4 slices cubed white bread
2 cups diced potatoes

2 cups sliced sausage
1 teaspoon salt
Dash of pepper
Butter

Line a good sized casserole with cabbage leaves. Mix the eggs and milk with egg beater. Add cubed bread. Cut rest of cabbage very fine. Mix cabbage, potatoes, sausage, salt, pepper, bread and egg-milk mixture. After well mixed put in casserole lined with cabbage. Dot with butter and bake 1 hour covered. Take lid off last 10 minutes to brown. Bake at 350 degrees.

Yield: 6 to 8 servings
Ann King Nies

CHICKEN SUPREME

1 small jar chipped beef
6 large ½ chicken breasts—boned
6 slices bacon

1 can mushroom soup
½ pint sour cream

Put layer of chipped beef in bottom of casserole. Wrap bacon around each chicken breast. Place on chipped beef. Mix 1 can mushroom soup and ½ pint sour cream and pour over chicken. Cover with foil and bake at 300 degrees for 3 hours.

Yield: 6 servings
Betty Wise

ITALIAN CHICKEN

1 broiler cut in quarters
Salt and pepper
Flour
¼ cup olive oil
¼ pound proscuitto, thinly sliced
4 to 5 small onions

1 green pepper minced
1 canned pimento, chopped
1 clove garlic, chopped
1 #1 can tomatoes
1 cup sliced mushrooms

Dredge chicken in salt, pepper, and flour. Brown in oil. Add all ingredients, except mushrooms, cover and simmer 1 hour. Add mushrooms, simmer 10 to 15 minutes. Serve over spaghetti.

Yield: 4 servings
Arnold Adams

STEAMED TURKEY

20 pound turkey
3 or 4 celery leaves
1 onion

1 carrot
Poultry seasoning
2 cups water

For use in salads or casserole. Place celery, onion, and carrot inside turkey cavity that has been lightly sprinkled with poultry seasoning. Place turkey breast down on rack in roasting pan in 350 degree oven. Add 2 cups water to pan. Cover and roast for 3 hours.

Yield: 26 cups meat
Regina Mueller

TRI-GAS BAR-B-CUE SAUCE

1 bottle Bar-B-Cue Sauce with
   onions
1 bottle chili sauce
1 bottle ketchup
1 bottle cooking sherry
1 bottle (5-ounce) soy sauce

1 bottle (7-ounce) Worcestershire
   sauce
1 pound box brown sugar
1 #2 can crushed pineapple
1 tablespoon liquid smoke

Mix in blender and simmer for 10 to 15 minutes to melt sugar. Mix well.

Yield: 12 cups

BARBECUE SAUCE
for chicken or leftover meats

1 medium onion chopped (½ cup)
½ cup chopped celery
2 tablespoons corn oil
2 tablespoons brown sugar
2 tablespoons vinegar
3 tablespoons Worcestershire
   sauce

1 cup catsup
1 cup water
3 tablespoons prepared mustard
Salt and pepper
Cayenne

Cook onion and celery until tender. Then add remaining ingredients and simmer 30 minutes.

Yield: 1 pint
Kay Everngam

CHICKEN BARBECUE SAUCE

½ cup salad oil
1 cup cider vinegar
2 tablespoons salt

¼ teaspoon black pepper
1½ teaspoons poultry seasoning
1 whole egg, well beaten

Mix all dry ingredients, add vinegar and well beaten egg, finally add oil. If mixture must stand, keep it in the refrigerator and shake well before using. Brush chicken before placing on grill and brush again each time they are turned. Enough sauce for 5 chicken halves.

Yield: 5 servings
Poultry Dept. of University of Md.

CUMBERLAND SAUCE FOR WILD GOOSE

1 8-ounce jar red currant jelly
½ cup port wine
1 teaspoon ginger

Juice from ½ orange
Juice from ½ lemon
Rind grated from ½ orange

Bring to boil and thicken with small amount of corn starch. Cool to room temperature and serve with goose. We like it better hot.

Yield: 1 to 1½ cups
Mildred James

CHEESE SOUFFLÉ SANDWICHES

8 slices white bread
8 slices American cheese
8 slices Cheddar cheese
3 eggs
1½ cups milk

Salt
Pepper
Butter
Parmesan cheese

Make 4 cheese sandwiches with bread and two types of cheese. Butter well on the outside and fit into square cake pan. Make batter of eggs, milk, salt, and pepper. Pour over sandwiches and let soak overnight if possible. Sprinkle with Parmesan cheese and bake at 350 degrees for 40 minutes.

These may be made with several additions: 1 can of crabmeat in sandwiches on top of cheese; 1 slice of ham; 2 slices of bacon; 1 slice of turkey or creamed shrimp poured over each sandwich at serving time.

Yield: 4 servings
Hettie Russell

TOMATO QUICHE

1 10-inch unbaked pie crust
Tomato slices ⅓ inch thick
3 eggs
½ pound Swiss cheese (cubed)
1¾ cups half and half

3 tablespoons chopped onion
1 tablespoon butter
½ teaspoon dried dill weed
1 teaspoon salt
Dash cayenne

Put tomatoes in bottom of pie crust—enough to cover pan. Sauté onions in butter till limp. Combine beaten eggs with cheese, cream, dill, salt, and onion. Pour into shell over tomatoes. Bake at 425 degrees for 10 minutes, lower heat to 325 degrees and bake 45 minutes longer or until firmly set. Let rest 10 minutes before cutting.

Yield: 6 servings
Kay Howell

QUICHE LORRAINE

1 9-inch unbaked pie shell, well
   chilled
1 tablespoon butter or margarine
4 eggs
2 cups milk

¾ teaspoon salt
Pinch nutmeg
⅛ teaspoon cayenne pepper
1 cup grated Swiss cheese

Rub butter over surface of pie shell. Combine eggs, milk, salt, nutmeg, cayenne pepper. Beat until mixed thoroughly. Sprinkle cheese in pie shell, pour milk mixture over cheese. Bake at 450 degrees for 15 minutes, reduce to 300 degrees and bake 40 minutes or until knife inserted comes out clean. Bacon or ham bits can be added.

Yield: 6-8 servings
Mary Jo Shaffer

SHAKE AND BAKE

4 cups dry bread crumbs
½ cup flour
1 tablespoon paprika
4 teaspoons salt

4 teaspoons sugar
4 teaspoons onion powder
1 teaspoon garlic powder
½ cup solid shortening

Mix dry ingredients and cut in shortening. Store in covered jar. Dip chicken or pork in milk, then shake in crumbs. Bake uncovered until tender.

Martha Shipe

BACON & EGG CASSEROLE

4 cups plain croutons
2 cups shredded Cheddar cheese
8 slightly beaten eggs
4 cups milk
1 teaspoon salt

1 teaspoon mustard
¼ teaspoon onion powder
Dash pepper
8 slices bacon

Grease rectangular casserole.

Combine croutons and cheese. Put in casserole. Combine eggs, milk, salt, mustard, onion powder, and pepper. Mix and pour over croutons and cheese. Cook 8 or more slices bacon. Crumble and sprinkle on top. Bake at 325 degrees 55 to 60 minutes (check at 45 minutes).

Yield: 10 to 12 servings
Kay Everngam

Plowing by horse or mule was made much easier for humans by the invention of the riding plow. Here, the first riding plow in Caroline County is tried out, about 1915.

VEGETABLES
and
ACCOMPANIMENTS

SOUR CREAM BAKED POTATOES

4 medium baking potatoes
1 cup sour cream
½ teaspoon ground cumin seeds
   (optional)

2 tablespoons butter or
   margarine
½ teaspoon salt
Dash of pepper

Scrub potatoes and prick with fork. Bake at 425 degrees for 50 to 60 minutes. Take thin slice from top of potatoes and discard; scoop out the center of potatoes and mix in bowl with other ingredients. Beat until fluffy—adding milk if necessary. Spoon mixture back into potato shells, sprinkle with paprika (or use cheese), bake at 375 degrees for 20 to 25 minutes until heated through. (Can be prepared ahead of time and kept in refrigerator, then the last baking time can be done at serving time).

Yield: 4 servings
Marianne Kent

PENNSYLVANIA DUTCH POTATO FILLING

6 to 8 medium potatoes, cooked
   and mashed
½ cup onion, diced
⅓ cup celery, diced
1 tablespoon flaked or fresh,
   chopped parsley

3 eggs, beaten
3 or 4 slices stale bread, cubed
Milk
Salt, pepper to taste
Paprika to taste

Sauté onion and celery. Place in bowl with potatoes. Add parsley, eggs, bread cubes. Moisten with milk. Add salt, pepper, paprika to taste. Mix well and bake in 350 degree oven for 1 hour, until puffed and golden.

Note: This is better made the day before serving, stored in refrigerator.

Yield: 8 servings
Courtesy: King Clan Cookbook
Carol Nies Buohl

POTATOES MARGARET

1 cup sour cream	2 tablespoons fine bread crumbs
½ cup milk	Salt
1 tablespoon instant minced onion	Pepper
5 cups sliced, cooked potatoes	1 tablespoon butter

Combine sour cream, milk, and onion. Grease 10x6x1½-inch baking dish. Place one-half of potatoes in dish, flavor with salt and pepper. Add ½ cream mixture. Repeat layers. Melt butter, add crumbs, and toss. Sprinkle over top. Bake at 350 degrees 20 to 25 minutes.

Yield: 6 servings
Ruth Evans

FRIED RICE

1 teaspoon monosodium glutamate	1 small onion, chopped
2 teaspoons cooking oil	2 tablespoons soy sauce
1 teaspoon salt	4 cups cold cooked rice
½ can bean sprouts, drained	4 slices crumbled bacon, or
2 eggs, beaten	1 cup diced ham, pork or shrimp
2 tablespoons green onion, chopped	

Cook beaten eggs as an omelet, set aside, and dice. Brown onion in oil, then add meat or shrimp, if used. Slowly add cold rice, bean sprouts, and salt. Pour soy sauce around outer edge of pan and mix with rice to uniform color. Cook slowly 3 minutes on medium heat. Add eggs, crumbled bacon, and monosodium glutamate. Heat 3 minutes longer. Serve hot.

Yield: 4-6 servings
Sonya Felipe

BAKED RICE

1 cup rice
3 tablespoons butter
1 teaspoon salt

3 cups cold water
3 bouillon cubes (chicken)
Chopped parsley

Mix all together in baking dish. Bake 2 hours at 300 degrees.

Yield: 4 servings
Betty Wise

CHEESE GRITS CASSEROLE

1½ cups grits
6 cups water
1 stick butter or margarine
2 cups sharp cheddar cheese,
    grated

3 teaspoons seasoned salt
1 cup milk
3 eggs, well beaten

Cook grits in water for 20 minutes. Add the remaining ingredients and turn into a greased 9x13-inch casserole. Bake for 1 hour at 375 degrees. Serve hot.

Yield: 8-10 servings
Virginia Warren

BLACK-EYED PEAS

2 #2 cans black-eyed peas
1 sweet onion, diced

½ teaspoon Worcestershire sauce
3 tablespoons bacon drippings

Drain half the liquid from the peas. Add remaining ingredients. Heat thoroughly. Serve hot.

Yield: 5 servings
R. Doris Stivers

VEGETABLES

FRIED OKRA

1 pound fresh small pods of okra,　½ cup yellow corn meal
　　cut in ½ inch pieces　　　　　Fat
1 teaspoon salt

Season okra with salt and mix well. Sprinkle corn meal over okra and mix thoroughly. Fry in deep hot fat until lightly browned. Drain on paper towel.

Yield: 4 to 6 servings
R. Doris Stivers

POKE SALLAT

16 stalks of poke weed not　　　Salt to taste
　　over 8 inches long　　　　　2 strips fat bacon or pork meat

Wash poke carefully and drop in kettle of boiling salted water. Cook covered, for ten minutes. Pour off all water. Cover poke with fresh water, salt slightly, add bacon cut in pieces and cook gently for ten minutes. Drain and serve.

Note: poke may be served without any meat, as a green vegetable.

Yield: 4 servings
Virginia Brown

FAR EAST CELERY

4 cups celery sliced ¼ inches　　1 small jar pimentos, diced
　　diagonally　　　　　　　　¼ cup sliced almonds
5 ounces water chestnuts, sliced　2 tablespoons melted butter
　　thin　　　　　　　　　　¼ cup crumb mixture
1 cup cream of chicken soup

Cook celery 8 minutes in salt water. Drain. Add chestnuts, pimentos, and soup. Pour into casserole, top with crumbs mixed in butter. Sprinkle almonds over top. Bake at 350 degrees for 20 to 25 minutes. Delicious!!

Yield: 8 servings
Dot Brown

CORN PUDDING

2 cups corn
1 tablespoon flour
3 tablespoons sugar
2 eggs

¾ teaspoon salt
¾ cup milk
¼ stick butter

Put in mixer or blender. Mix well. Bake in well greased baking dish for 45 minutes at 375 degrees.

Yield: 6 servings
Florence F. Nuttle

SOUTHERN CORN PUDDING

3 cups cream style corn
1 teaspoon salt
3 tablespoons sugar
1 tablespoon cornstarch

6 tablespoons melted butter
5 eggs, well beaten
2½ cups milk

Stir into corn: salt, sugar, butter, cornstarch, well-beaten eggs, milk. Place in buttered baking dish, set in shallow pan with a little water. Do not let bottom become brown. Bake 45 minutes to one hour at 375 degrees, or until pudding is solid.

Yield: 10 servings
Mary Jo Shaffer

VIRGINIA PUDDING

1 cup corn, cut from cob,
    or frozen
2 cups milk
2 eggs

1½ tablespoons butter, melted
1 teaspoon baking powder
⅛ teaspoon white pepper
½ teaspoon salt

Beat eggs lightly. Add milk, corn, baking powder, seasoning. Add melted butter. Mix well, turn into buttered baking dish or individual ramekins. Bake 30 minutes in 350 degree oven for large dish, 15 to 20 minutes for small.

Yield: 6 servings
Elsie King

CAULIFLOWER WITH BROWN CRUMBS

1 head of cauliflower—about 3 pounds	¾ cup bread crumbs
	6 tablespoons butter
Basic cream sauce	⅛ teaspoon paprika

Wash cauliflower and separate into florets. May be cooked whole if desired. Brown crumbs in butter, add paprika.

Make basic white sauce (see recipe in section on sauces).

Place cauliflower on heat-proof platter, spread sauce over top. Sprinkle crumb mixture on top. Broil for 2 to 5 minutes until crumbs and sauce are bubbly. A dusting of Parmesan cheese before placing under broiler adds a nice flavor.

Yield: 5 to 8 servings
Hannah Adams

Plant all underground crops in the dark of the moon, all crops above the ground in the light of the moon.

MARINATED TOMATOES

10 to 12 tomatoes, peeled, and sliced	1 tablespoon minced fresh basil
1 red onion, thinly sliced	1 teaspoon salt
½ cup olive oil	½ teaspoon dry mustard
⅓ cup wine vinegar	½ teaspoon freshly ground pepper
2 teaspoons oregano or	2 cloves garlic, minced

Combine tomatoes and onion. Combine rest of ingredients and pour over tomatoes and onion. Cover and refrigerate 2 to 4 hours, basting occasionally.

Yield: 8 to 10 servings
Margaret R. Myers

DRIED BEANS

1 pound dried beans
Salt pork or ham hock

¼ teaspoon sugar
⅛ teaspoon baking powder

Wash and pick beans. Place in pot with salt pork or ham hock. Add sugar and baking powder. Bring to boil, uncovered. Boil vigorously until water is reduced almost to top of the beans. Add *boiling* water to 2½ inches above the beans. Cook until water is reduced about 1 inch—boiling fast. Salt. Turn heat to low and put lid on. Let cook until tender—45 minutes to 1 hour. For pintos, cook 45 minutes.

Yield: 12 servings
R. Doris Stivers

GREEN LIMA BEAN CASSEROLE

8 strips of bacon
2 cups green lima beans, cooked
1½ cups chopped onion

½ cup chopped celery
1½ cups shredded Monterey Jack
cheese

Fry bacon and drain on paper towels. Crumble and reserve. Pour off all but 2 tablespoons bacon fat. Sauté onion and celery in the 2 tablespoons bacon fat. Add lima beans and cheese and toss together. Place in casserole and sprinkle with crumbled bacon. Bake one-half hour at 350 degrees.

Yield: 6 servings
Chester Nelson

CANDIED CARROTS WITH ORANGE JUICE

12 to 15 carrots (can be cooked
the day before, leave whole)
½ cup brown sugar
½ cup sugar

1 tablespoon cornstarch
1 cup orange juice
1 tablespoon orange rind
2 or 3 tablespoons butter

Cook ingredients and pour over carrots. Bake in 325 degree oven for 1 hour. Baste frequently.

Yield: 10 to 12 servings
Dolly Moore

PIQUANT CARROTS

¾ cup liquid (water or carrot juice)
1 tablespoon cornstarch
1 tablespoon powdered orange drink
2 tablespoons butter

2 1-pound cans whole carrots (or equivalent fresh cooked)
Dash salt
Nutmeg—dash
Chopped parsley

Mix liquid, corn starch, and orange powder. Boil until thickened. Add 2 tablespoons butter and carrots. Add salt and nutmeg. Heat until carrots are hot. Stir to prevent sticking. Serve with chopped parsley.

Yield: 6 to 8 servings
Nancy Adams

GRYZBY @'SMIETANIE
(MUSHROOMS WITH SOUR CREAM)
Polish Dish

1¼ pounds mushrooms, sliced
¾ pint sour cream
6 tablespoons butter
1 onion, chopped

Salt
Pepper
A little paprika
2 tablespoons milk

Chop onion and brown in butter; sprinkle with flour, brown and add the milk gradually. Bring to a boil and add mushrooms. Season with salt, pepper and paprika. Simmer and add half the sour cream. Cook very gently until mushrooms are tender. Before serving, stir in remaining sour cream. Sprinkle with more paprika. Serve with meat or use as an Hors d'Oeuvre.

Yield: 4-6 servings
Mrs. Howard W. Reardon

SQUASH CASSEROLE

½ cup butter or margarine
4 cups thinly diced zucchini
4 cups thinly sliced yellow
   squash

½ cup soft bread crumbs
¼ cup grated Parmesan cheese
½ cup bottled barbecue sauce

In a large skillet with cover, sauté zucchini in ¼ cup butter or margarine, stirring frequently until slices are transparent. Set aside. In remaining butter or margarine, sauté yellow squash. Return zucchini to pan. Pour barbecue sauce over vegetables; toss until evenly mixed. Heat until steaming hot, then place in a broiler-proof dish. Sprinkle with bread crumbs, then cheese. Broil 5 inches from heat 1 or 2 minutes, until crumbs are golden.

Yield: 6-8 servings
Regina Mueller

SPINACH PUDDING

2 10-ounce packages chopped
   spinach
2 tablespoons butter
1½ cups shredded Swiss cheese
Dash pepper
2 12-ounce cans mushrooms,
   drained

1½ cups milk
4 eggs, beaten slightly
1 teaspoon salt
2 tablespoons chopped onion
Nutmeg

Cook and drain spinach. Heat milk and butter until hot. Combine all ingredients. Put in buttered casserole. Sprinkle nutmeg on top. Put casserole in hot water and bake in slow oven at 325 degrees for 60 minutes.

Yield: 8 servings
Mrs. Dolly Moore

RATATOUILLE

2 garlic cloves, minced
1 onion sliced thin
½ cup olive oil
1 medium eggplant, diced
3 medium zucchini, sliced

1 green pepper, sliced
3½ cups tomatoes
1 tablespoon oregano or basil
Salt
Pepper

Sauté garlic and onion in oil until clear. Add eggplant and toss. Add zucchini and pepper and cook for 10 minutes. Add remaining ingredients and simmer, covered, for 30 minutes. Uncover and simmer 30 minutes longer.

Yield: 6 servings
Betty Wise

EGGPLANT PARMESAN
(low calorie)

1½ pounds eggplant
1 medium green pepper, sliced
2 tablespoons chopped onion
1½ cups tomato juice
½ teaspoon garlic salt
½ teaspoon oregano
¼ teaspoon salt

½ teaspoon sugar
2 gratings black pepper
2 tablespoons grated Parmesan
   cheese
½ cup shredded low fat
   mozzarella cheese

Peel eggplant and slice about ¾-inch thick. Place slices in 8-inch square pan or casserole. Cover with green pepper and onion. Mix tomato juice and seasonings. Pour over all. Bake at 400 degrees until eggplant is tender, about 35 minutes. Mix the two cheeses and sprinkle on top. Bake 5 to 10 more minutes, until cheese is melted.

Yield: 6 servings
Sara Kidd

ROMAN EGGPLANT

1 medium eggplant, pared and
   cut into ½ inch slices
½ cup butter, or margarine,
   melted
1 8-ounce can (about 1 cup)
   spaghetti sauce with
   mushrooms

1 tablespoon crushed oregano
   leaves
¾ cup fine dry bread crumbs
1 cup shredded sharp American
   or mozzarella cheese

Dip eggplant in butter, then in mixture of bread crumbs and salt. Place on a greased cookie sheet. Spoon sauce on each slice, sprinkle with oregano and cheese. Bake in hot oven, 450 degrees, 10 to 12 minutes, or until done.

Yield: 4 or 5 servings
Grace Bamford

BAKED CRUSHED PINEAPPLE

3 eggs
2 tablespoons flour
½ cup sugar
⅓ teaspoon salt

1 #2 can crushed pineapple
¼ pound butter, melted
3 slices bread, cut or
   broken fine

Blend eggs, flour, sugar, and salt together. Add crushed pineapple and blend. Grease baking dish, pour mixture in. Sprinkle bread on top; pour melted butter over all. Bake 35 minutes in 350 degree oven.

Yield: 12 servings
Caroline Wheatley

BAKED PINEAPPLE

1 package instant imitation eggs
  (or 2 beaten eggs)
½ cup sugar
2 tablespoons flour
1 20-ounce can crushed pineapple

4 slices bread, broken into small
  pieces
4 tablespoons melted butter or
  margarine

Combine first five ingredients and pour into buttered casserole. Cover with melted butter. Bake for 40 minutes at 350 degrees.

Yield: 6 servings
Laura Rogers

SCALLOPED APPLES

6 large apples
¼ teaspoon cinnamon
¼ teaspoon salt
1 tablespoon lemon juice

¼ cup water
¾ cup sugar
¼ cup flour
⅓ cup butter

Pare, core, slice apples. Put in shallow buttered baking dish. Pour cinnamon, salt, lemon juice, and water mixture over apples. Mix sugar, flour, and butter until crumbly and put on top. Bake for 30 minutes or more in 400 degree oven. Serve as vegetable dish with pork, chicken or ham.

Note: This is a favorite old Kent County recipe.

Yield: 6 servings
Caroline Allaband

CRYSTAL APPLE RINGS

4 large apples, cored, sliced   4 tablespoons butter or
     ½-inch thick   margarine
2 tablespoons sugar

Melt butter in skillet and add sugar. Stir until slightly carmelized. Add apple rings and sauté over low heat until golden brown on both sides.

Note: Pineapple slices, cooked sweet potato slices, orange sections, or halved bananas may be cooked this way. A perfect garnish for roast pork.

Yield: 6 servings
Helene Thawley

Melons were and are one of the prides of Caroline County farmers. This family is shown preparing for a summer picnic in Caroline County right around the turn of the century.

DESSERTS

APPLE BUTTER CAKE

1 cup sugar
½ cup butter
4 beaten eggs
2 cups flour
1 teaspoon soda

1 teaspoon cinnamon
1 teaspoon cloves
4 teaspoons sour milk
1 cup apple butter

Cream sugar and butter. Add beaten eggs. Mix dry ingredients. Add some flour mixture to first mixture. Then add sour milk and remaining flour. Beat smooth. Lastly add 1 cup thick apple butter. Bake in two pans at 350 degrees for about 30 minutes or until done, or try with broom straw. Cool. Spread with white or caramel icing.

Yield: 12-16 servings
Elinor Pearson Towers

APPLESAUCE CAKE

½ cup lard
1 cup raisins
1 cup sugar
1 cup sweetened applesauce
1 teaspoon baking soda
2 tablespoons hot water
1 cup nuts

1 egg
2 cups flour
1 teaspoon cinnamon
½ teaspoon allspice
½ teaspoon nutmeg
½ teaspoon salt

Cream lard and sugar. Add applesauce and beaten egg. Sift dry ingredients and add to creamed mixture with hot water. Mix well and fold in raisins and nuts. Bake at 350 degrees in greased and floured tube pan for 1 hour or until cake tests done.

Yield: 1 cake—24 to 30 slices
Submitted by Mrs. Wilbert Merriken
(Recipe of Mrs. Edith Merriken)

LOW CALORIE APPLESAUCE CAKE

2 cups flour
1 cup sugar
1 teaspoon cinnamon
½ teaspoon nutmeg
¼ teaspoon cloves

2 teaspoons baking soda
2 cups raisins
½ cup cooking oil
1 pound can applesauce

Mix all ingredients together and pour into a greased and floured tube pan. Bake in a 350 degree oven for 45 minutes. Cool in pan about 10 minutes. May be iced or just covered with a mixture of lemon juice and powdered sugar.

Yield: 12 to 15 slices
Louise Crouse

APPLE TEA-CAKE

1½ cups all-purpose flour
2 teaspoons baking powder
¼ teaspoon salt
⅓ cup soft butter
1 cup sugar

1 teaspoon vanilla
2 eggs
½ cup evaporated milk
1 large red Delicious apple
½ cup coarsely chopped walnuts

Stir together fork-stirred all purpose flour, baking powder, salt. Cream butter, sugar and vanilla. Beat in eggs, one at a time, until blended. Add flour mixture, evaporated milk (undiluted), unpeeled apple and diced (¼ inch), and chopped walnuts. Stir just until dry ingredients are moistened. Line bottom of 9x5x3-inch loaf pan with wax paper. Grease paper. Turn into prepared pan. Bake in pre-heated 350 degree oven until a cake tester comes out clean—about 65 minutes. Loosen edges and turn out on wire rack. Turn right side up; cool completely. Store in refrigerator in foil. Warm before serving if desired.

Yield: 1 loaf cake
Mary McHarry

APPLE DAPPLE CAKE

3 eggs
1½ cups vegetable oil
2 cups sugar
3 cups flour
1 teaspoon salt
1 teaspoon baking soda

1 teaspoon cinnamon
2 teaspoons vanilla
¼ cup milk
3 cups raw chopped apples
1 cup chopped nuts

Mix oil, eggs, and sugar together. Then add the remaining ingredients, leaving the apples and nuts until last. Put into a greased-floured 9x13-inch pan and bake 1 hour at 350 degrees.

TOPPING FOR APPLE DAPPLE CAKE

1 stick margarine
¼ cup milk

1 cup brown sugar

Cook 2½ minutes. Pour over hot cake.

Yield: 18 servings
Ginger Snyder

APPLE FOOD CAKE

1 cup oil
2 cups sugar
2 well beaten eggs
3 cups sifted flour
½ teaspoon salt

1 teaspoon soda
2 teaspoons vanilla
2 teaspoons cinnamon
3 cups chopped raw apples
1 cup chopped pecans

Mix together the oil, sugar, and beaten eggs. Then add the flour, salt, soda, vanilla, and cinnamon. Mix well and add the apples and pecans. Bake 1½ hours at 325 degrees in a greased tube pan.

Yield: 1 tube cake
Betty S. Potter

CARROT CAKE

2 cups sugar
2½ cups flour
1 teaspoon salt
1 teaspoon cinnamon
½ teaspoon nutmeg
2 teaspoons baking powder

2 teaspoons baking soda
1½ cups cooking oil
4 eggs
3 cups grated raw carrots
1 cup chopped nuts

Mix dry ingredients and sift into large bowl. Add oil and mix. Add well beaten eggs. Fold in carrots and nuts. Put in greased tube pan. Bake at 325 degrees about 1½ hours or until cake tests clean. Serve plain or with cream cheese icing.

CREAM CHEESE ICING

1 8-ounce package cream
    cheese softened

1 tablespoon butter softened
1 pound powdered sugar

In medium bowl with electric mixer at medium speed, beat cheese with butter until creamy. Add powdered sugar; beat until light and fluffy. Spread thickly over top of cake.

Yield: 18 to 20 slices
Kay Howell

CARROT CAKE

2 small jars of carrots (baby
    food)
1½ cups salad oil
2 cups sugar
2½ cups flour
1 teaspoon baking soda
1 teaspoon baking powder

1 teaspoon nutmeg
1 teaspoon cinnamon
1 teaspoon salt
4 tablespoons hot water
1 cup walnuts
4 eggs separated

Mix all ingredients, except egg whites. Whip egg whites and fold in. Pour into tube pan which has been greased well, or bake in 2 layers. Bake at 350 degrees 1 hour in tube pan, ½ hour in layers. Cool, frost with a cream cheese frosting.

Yield: 1 tube cake or 1 2-layer cake
Pauline Myers

BOILED CAKE

1 cup raisins
4 cups brown sugar (2 pounds)
2 cups vegetable shortening
4 cups hot water
½ cup chopped nuts

1 teaspoon cloves
1 teaspoon cinnamon
1 teaspoon salt
2 teaspoons baking soda
7½ cups sifted flour

Boil all ingredients except for the baking soda and flour for 20 minutes. Cool several hours or overnight. Add sifted flour and soda. Mix thoroughly. Bake in moderate 325 degree oven for 1 hour and 10 minutes (35 minutes on lower shelf and 35 minutes on upper shelf).

Note: Grease pans (7⁷/₈x3⁷/₈x2½ inches), place waxed paper in bottom; grease paper and flour lightly. Be sure to cool in pans for about 10 minutes. Use knife around edge to loosen and invert on rack to cool. Wrap and store in refrigerator. Keeps very well.

Yield: 6 loaves
Laura S. Rogers

DUMP CAKE

1 package yellow cake mix
1 can crushed pineapple
2 sticks margarine
4 cups sliced fresh raw apples
2 teaspoons lemon juice

2 tablespoons cornstarch
¾ cup chopped nuts
1 teaspoon cinnamon
½ teaspoon nutmeg

Dump pineapple and juice in large pyrex dish (9x13). Mix apples with lemon juice, corn starch, cinnamon, and nutmeg. Spread over pineapple. Sprinkle dry cake mix over top. Sprinkle with nuts. Slice margarine or butter in thin pats and cover entire pan. Bake one hour at 350 degrees. Serve warm, with whipped cream, if desired. (May be made day before and heated).

Yield: 15 servings
Kay Everngam

CHOCOLATE CAKE

3½ tablespoons cocoa	2 cups flour
1 stick margarine	2 eggs
½ cup vegetable oil	½ cup buttermilk
1 cup water	1 teaspoon soda
2 cups sugar	1 teaspoon salt

Bring to a boil the cocoa, margarine, vegetable oil, and water. Add the sugar and flour. Then add the remaining ingredients. Pour into an ungreased baking dish (9x12). Bake at 400 degrees for 25 minutes.

CHOCOLATE FUDGE ICING

3½ tablespoons cocoa	1 lb. powdered sugar
½ stick margarine	1 teaspoon vanilla
½ cup milk	

Bring to a boil the cocoa, margarine and milk. Add the sugar and vanilla and pour over hot cake.

Yield: 1 cake (cross between cake and brownies)
Ex-Lieutenant Governor Samuel W. Bogley
and Mrs. Rita Bogley
State of Maryland
Annapolis, Maryland

GRANDMOTHER'S 1½ CAKE

1½ cups cake flour	Melted butter
1 cup sugar	Milk
2 teaspoons baking powder	½ teaspoon vanilla
1 egg plus 1 egg yolk	

Sift flour, sugar, and baking powder into bowl. In a one cup measure break the one egg and add egg yolk. Reserve white for frosting. Fill cup to half with melted butter, then to top with milk. Make well in flour mixture and add contents of cup. Add vanilla and beat vigorously. Bake in 8x8-inch pan for 45 minutes at 350 degrees.

Yield: 16 2-inch squares
Carol Stockley

OLD FASHIONED DARK FRUIT CAKE

1 pound butter, creamed
1 dozen eggs, separated
1 pound sugar
1 pound flour
4 1-pound boxes raisins or 2
    1-pound boxes raisins and 2
    1-pound boxes of currants
4 ounces lemon peel
4 ounces orange peel

¼ pound citron
½ pound figs
3 teaspoons cinnamon
2 teaspoons allspice
2 teaspoons cloves
2 teaspoons nutmeg
1 pint liquid (rum, wine or
    whiskey)

Cream butter and sugar; add beaten egg yolks. Sift flour and spices together and add to creamed mixture. Cut figs small and add to other fruits, mixing with ¾-1 cup flour. Add to above mixture. Stir in liquid. Fold in well beaten egg whites last. Bake in two tube pans lined with greased brown paper. Or, use 4 large loaf pans or 8 small loaf pans. Baking time—3 hours at 300 degrees for tube pans; 2 hours at 300 degrees for large loaf pans; 1 hour at 300 degrees for small loaf pans.

Make several weeks in advance. Wrap in cheesecloth soaked in whiskey, rum or brandy, or they may be wrapped in plastic wrap and foil. Store in covered container. Liquid may be added at intervals. Keeps indefinitely and is very moist.

Yield: 10 pounds of cake
Kay Everngam

CHEESECAKE

Crust:

1¾ cups graham cracker crumbs   ½ teaspoon cinnamon
¼ cup walnuts, chopped   ½ cup melted butter

Mix together (reserve 3 tablespoons for topping). Press into bottom and side of a 9-inch spring form pan.

Filling:

3 eggs   2 8-ounce packages cream cheese
1 cup sugar   2 teaspoons vanilla
3 cups sour cream

Combine eggs, cheese, sugar and vanilla. Beat until smooth. Blend in sour cream. Pour into pan and top with reserved crumbs. Bake at 375 degrees for 1 hour. Chill 4-5 hours.

Yield: 12 servings
Sonya Felipe

FUDGE CAKE

2 sticks margarine   1½ cups nuts
½ cup cocoa   Dash salt
4 eggs   1 package miniature
1½ cups flour   marshmallows
2 cups sugar

Melt margarine, add sugar, mix well. Add beaten eggs one at a time. Add dry ingredients, mix well, fold in nuts. Pour in a greased and floured 9x13-inch pan. Bake at 350 degrees for 30 minutes.

Remove from oven and cover with marshmallows. Return to oven and melt marshmallows (partially), do not let them burn. Make icing using ingredients below:

1 box confectioners sugar   ½ cup milk
⅓ cup cocoa   1 teaspoon vanilla
½ stick margarine, melted

Mix ingredients, spoon over cake while cake is still hot. You may also use regular chocolate frosting, but frost cake after it has cooled.

Yield: 1 cake
Mary Jo Shaffer

ARKANSAS FUDGE CAKE

½ cup butter
2 cups sugar
4 squares chocolate
2 eggs
2 cups flour

2 teaspoons baking powder
½ teaspoon salt
1½ cups milk
2 teaspoons vanilla
1 cup chopped pecans

Cream butter and sugar. Add melted chocolate and beaten eggs. Sift dry ingredients and add alternately with milk. Add vanilla and nuts and bake in a 9x13-inch greased and floured pan. Bake at 350 degrees for 45 minutes.

ICING

1 cup butter
4 ounces chocolate (4 squares)
2 eggs
3 cups powdered sugar

⅛ teaspoon salt
1 teaspoon lemon juice
2 cups nuts

Melt butter and chocolate together. Add beaten eggs, sugar, salt, vanilla, and lemon juice. Mix part of nuts in icing and sprinkle others on top of cake.

Mary Jo Shaffer

JANET'S SAUERKRAUT CAKE

⅔ cup margarine
1½ cups white sugar
3 eggs
2¼ cups flour
1 teaspoon soda
1 teaspoon baking powder

About 1 teaspoon salt
½ cup cocoa
1 cup cold water
⅔ cup drained and rinsed
   sauerkraut (chopped)

Cream butter and sugar together. Add eggs. Sift dry ingredients and add to the creamed mixture alternately with the cold water. Fold in sauerkraut last. Bake at 350 degrees in 8x8-inch pan for about 30 minutes or until done.

Yield: one 8x8-inch cake
Janet Challman Johnson

ITALIAN CREAM CAKE

2 cups sugar
1 stick margarine
½ cup shortening
1 teaspoon vanilla
5 egg yolks—beaten

2 cups all purpose flour
1 teaspoon soda
1 cup buttermilk
5 egg whites beaten
1 cup flaked coconut

Cream sugar, margarine, shortening. Add vanilla. Beat until light and fluffy. Add egg yolks. Blend. Mix flour and soda—alternate with buttermilk. Fold in beaten egg whites and coconut. Bake in 3 8-inch prepared round pans at 350 degrees for 30 to 35 minutes.

ICING

1 package (8-ounce) cream
    cheese
1 stick margarine
1 box confectioners sugar

1 teaspoon vanilla
1 cup chopped nuts
Chopped maraschino cherries
    (optional)

Combine first 4 ingredients and blend thoroughly. Add nuts and cherries.

Yield: 1 3-layer cake
Sonya Felipe

AARON'S BUNDLES

1 cup sugar
½ cup butter or margarine
1 egg
2 tablespoons molasses
2½ cups sifted flour

1 teaspoon cinnamon
1 teaspoon nutmeg
1 teaspoon soda
1 cup milk

Cream together: sugar and butter or margarine. Add egg and molasses. Then add flour sifted with cinnamon, nutmeg, and soda. Mix alternately with 1 cup of milk. Grease small or medium size muffin pans and fill ⅔ full. Bake in moderate oven—350 degrees—for 20 to 30 minutes.

Yield: 2½ dozen, if small
Mary McHarry

SAUERKRAUT CAKE

2¼ cups sifted flour
1 teaspoon baking powder
1 teaspoon baking soda
¼ teaspoon salt
½ cup unsweetened cocoa
⅔ cup butter
1½ cups sugar

3 eggs
1 teaspoon vanilla
1 cup water
⅔ cup rinsed, drained and
    chopped sauerkraut
Mocha whipped cream

Grease and flour two 8-inch round cake pans. Sift together flour, baking powder, baking soda, salt and cocoa. In large bowl, cream butter and sugar. Thoroughly beat in eggs one at a time, and the vanilla. Stir in dry ingredients in 4 additions alternately with water, until smooth each time; begin and end with dry ingredients. Stir in sauerkraut. Turn into prepared pans. Bake in preheated 350 degree oven until cake tester comes out clean—about 30 minutes. Place on wire rack to cool for 10 minutes. Turn out onto wire racks to cool completely. Fill and frost with Mocha Whipped Cream. Store in refrigerator.

MOCHA WHIPPED CREAM

1½ cups heavy cream
3 tablespoons sugar

1 tablespoon instant coffee
2 teaspoons unsweetened cocoa

Whip cream, sugar, coffee and cocoa until soft peaks form. Frost cake.

Yield: 1 2-layer cake
Kay Howell

JEWEL CAKE

1½ cups graham cracker crumbs
⅓ cup sugar
½ cup melted margarine
1 3-ounce package strawberry
  gelatin
1 3-ounce package black cherry
  gelatin
1 3-ounce package lemon gelatin

½ cup sugar
1 9-ounce can crushed pineapple
2 tablespoons lemon juice
1½ cups whipped cream
Dash salt
3 cups hot water
1½ cups cold water
Walnuts

Mix graham cracker crumbs, sugar, and margarine together and press into bottom of 2½-inch high cake pan, chill. Dissolve strawberry gelatin in 1 cup hot water. Add ½ cup cold water and pour into 8-inch square pan. Chill firm. Dissolve black cherry gelatin in 1 cup hot water. Add ½ cup cold water and pour into a second 8-inch square pan. Chill firm. In large bowl dissolve lemon gelatin in 1 cup hot water. Add ½ cup cold water. Add sugar, crushed pineapple, ½ cup cold water, lemon juice, and salt. Chill partially and whip until fluffy.

Fold in chilled clear gelatin (which has been cut in ½-inch cubes) and whipped cream. Pour into crumb pan. Cover with walnuts and put in refrigerator for four hours.

Yield: 16 servings
Jean Dwyer

ZUCCHINI LOAF CAKE

2 cups sugar
1 cup cooking oil
3 eggs
3 cups flour
1 teaspoon baking soda
1 teaspoon baking powder

1 teaspoon salt
2 teaspoons cinnamon
1 teaspoon allspice
½ cup black walnuts
2 cups grated zucchini squash

In a large mixing bowl cream 2 cups sugar, and 1 cup oil. Add 3 eggs and beat well. Mix dry ingredients, and nuts, with wooden spoon. Add alternately with squash. Bake in greased and floured bread pans (2). Bake at 325 degrees for 1 hour, or until pick is clean when inserted in cake. Turn out of pan at once. Freezes well.

Yield: 2 loaves
Jane Johnson States

PEACHES & CREAM CAKE

¾ cup flour
1 teaspoon baking powder
½ teaspoon salt
1 small box regular vanilla
  pudding
½ cup milk
1 egg

3 tablespoons butter
Large size canned peaches, or
  use fresh
8-ounce softened cream cheese
3 tablespoons peach juice
½ cup sugar
1 tablespoon cinnamon

Cook in pie pan!
   Blend first 7 ingredients for 2 minutes. Put in greased 9-inch pie pan. Arrange peach slices on top. Blend cream cheese, juice and ½ cup sugar. Beat until creamy and place in center of peaches and spread out until 1 inch from edge of pan. Sprinkle with cinnamon mixed with 1 tablespoon sugar. Bake at 350 degrees for 25-30 minutes.

Yield: 1 9-inch pie
Bette Serviss

SOUR CREAM POUND CAKE

½ pound butter
2½ cups sugar
6 large eggs
3 cups flour

¼ teaspoon soda
½ teaspoon salt
1 cup sour cream
2 teaspoons vanilla

Sift flour, soda, and salt together. Cream butter and sugar with electric mixer. Add eggs one at a time, beating thoroughly. Add sifted dry ingredients alternately with sour cream. Beat 5 minutes at medium speed.
   Bake in large tube pan, greased, and floured for 1½ hours at 325 degrees, or use two loaf pans and bake for one hour. Cool cake thoroughly and wrap tightly in foil or plastic wrap. Refrigerate for at least three days before cutting. Cut cake cold but allow slices to come to room temperature before serving. This cake freezes well. The slices are delicious when lightly toasted.

Yield: 24 to 30 slices
Mary Wharton

TOMATO SOUP CAKE

2 cups sifted flour
1 teaspoon baking soda
2 teaspoons baking powder
1 teaspoon cinnamon
½ teaspoon cloves
1 teaspoon nutmeg

½ cup shortening
1 cup sugar
1 cup condensed tomato soup
1 cup chopped walnut meats
1 cup raisins

Sift flour, soda, baking powder, and spices together three times. Cream shortening with sugar until fluffy. Add sifted dry ingredients and tomato soup alternately in small amounts, beating thoroughly after each addition. Stir in nuts and raisins. Pour into small greased tube or loaf pan and bake in moderate oven (350 degrees), 50 to 60 minutes. Let stand 24 hours before cutting. Frost with cream cheese icing.

Yield: 1 tube cake
Kay Howell

DUVALL CAKE—1882

1 cup butter
2 cups sugar
4 eggs
1 cup sweet milk

1 lemon (juice and grated rind)
3 cups flour
1 teaspoon baking soda
1 teaspoon yeast powder

Cream thoroughly butter and sugar. Add eggs, beaten one at a time. Add lemon. Beat. Add last 2 ingredients sifted with flour, adding alternately with milk. Bake in 3 layers.

FILLING

5 apples grated
1 lemon (juice and rind)
1 cup sugar

1 egg
1 tablespoon butter

Combine all ingredients in saucepan. Let come to boil and cook 5 minutes. Cool, beat, and spread between layers. Sprinkle top with powdered sugar.

Yield: 1 3-layer cake
Susan Duvall

MILK 'N' HONEY CAKE

½ cup vegetable shortening
½ teaspoon salt
½ teaspoon vanilla
½ cup sugar
2 eggs, unbeaten

2 cups sifted flour (cake flour
    preferred)
2½ teaspoons baking powder
½ cup evaporated milk
½ cup honey

Combine shortening, salt and vanilla. Add sugar gradually and cream until light and fluffy. Add eggs, one at a time, beating thoroughly after each addition. Sift flour and baking powder together 3 times. Combine milk and honey. Add small amounts of flour to creamed mixture, alternately with combined milk and honey, beating after each addition until smooth. Pour batter into 8x8x2-inch pan, greased and floured. Bake in moderate oven (350 degrees) 50 to 60 minutes. Spread white fudge icing on top and sides of cake. May also be baked in two 8-inch layer pans in moderate oven (350 degrees) for 25 minutes.

WHITE FUDGE ICING

3 tablespoons vegetable
    shortening
1 tablespoon butter
5 tablespoons top milk, scalded

3 cups sifted confectioners sugar
1 teaspoon vanilla
¼ teaspoon salt

Melt vegetable shortening and butter in scalded top milk. Pour hot milk over sugar and stir until sugar is dissolved. Add vanilla and salt. Beat until smooth and thick enough to spread. Makes enough icing to cover top and sides of 10x10x2-inch cake or 1½ dozen cup cakes.

Mrs. Helene Thawley

HOT MILK CAKE

3 eggs
2 cups flour
½ cup butter
2 cups sugar

2½ teaspoons baking powder
2 teaspoons vanilla
1 cup milk

Beat eggs. Gradually add sugar. Sift flour and baking powder together and add to eggs. Heat milk and butter to almost hot and add. Bake in 13x9 inch greased cake pan at 375 degrees for 35 minutes.

TOPPING FOR HOT MILK CAKE

6 tablespoons brown sugar
4 tablespoons milk

6 tablespoons butter
1 can flaked coconut

Heat until blended. Add 1 can flaked coconut. Mix well. Spread over cake evenly. Place under broiler four minutes until golden brown.

Yield: 15-18 servings
Mildred James

PEANUT BLOSSOMS

1¾ cups flour,
1 teaspoon soda
½ teaspoon salt
½ cup butter
½ cup peanut butter

½ cup sugar
½ cup brown sugar
1 unbeaten egg
1 teaspoon vanilla
Chocolate kisses (1 package)

Cream ½ cup butter and ½ cup peanut butter and gradually add ½ cup sugar and ½ cup brown sugar. Add 1 unbeaten egg and 1 teaspoon vanilla. Add dry ingredients. Shape dough into balls and roll in granulated sugar. Place on ungreased cookie sheet and bake 8 minutes. Remove from oven and place a chocolate kiss on top of each cookie (press down firm). Return to oven 2 minutes until light brown. Bake at 350 degrees.

Yield: 4 dozen
Phyllis Garey

ALMOND BARK BARS

1 cup butter
1½ cups brown sugar
2 eggs
1 teaspoon vanilla
2¼ cups flour
2 cups quick oatmeal
1 teaspoon soda
½ teaspoon salt

1 pound white confectioners bark
1 (14-ounce) can sweetened
   condensed milk
3 tablespoons butter
¾ cup sliced almonds
1 teaspoon vanilla
¼ teaspoon almond extract

Cream butter, sugar, eggs, and vanilla. Combine flour, oatmeal, soda, salt. Blend into creamed mixture. Spread ⅔ of mixture onto greased 9x13-inch oblong baking pan. Bake in a 350 degree oven for 10 minutes. Melt confectioners bark, sweetened condensed milk, and butter in heavy bottom saucepan over low heat, add almonds and extract, pour evenly over partially baked crust. Drop remaining dough by teaspoonfuls on top of almond layer. Bake in a 350 degree oven for 25 minutes. Cool several hours before cutting into squares.

Yield: 4½ dozen
Maria Felipe

APPLE DREAM BARS

1½ cups flour
½ cup sugar
½ cup margarine
2 to 3 cups sliced apples
½ cup sugar
½ teaspoon cinnamon

3 eggs
1 cup brown sugar
¼ teaspoon salt
½ cup coconut
½ cup nuts chopped
2 tablespoons flour

Mix together the 1½ cups flour, ½ cup sugar and ½ cup margarine. Spread in an ungreased 8x10 pan. Arrange sliced apples over the first layer and sprinkle with second ½ cup sugar and cinnamon. Bake 30 minutes or until apples are done in moderate oven 350 degrees. While baking, mix eggs, brown sugar, salt, coconut, nuts and 2 tablespoons flour. Spread on hot layer and bake 20 minutes longer at 350 degrees. Cool and cut into bars.

Yield: 20 bars
Louise Schwartz

CHEWY PICNIC BARS

1 cup sifted flour
½ cup firmly packed brown
   sugar
½ cup butter
2 eggs
1 cup firmly packed brown
   sugar

1 teaspoon vanilla
1 tablespoon flour
½ teaspoon baking powder
¼ teaspoon salt
1 cup chopped nuts
1 cup shredded coconut
½ cup chopped dates or raisins

Mix the 1 cup of flour with ½ cup brown sugar. Cut in butter as for pastry. Press firmly into lightly greased 9x13-inch pan. Bake at 350 degrees for 12 minutes. Beat eggs, add remaining brown sugar. Beat until light and fluffy. Stir in vanilla and cook for 5 minutes.

   Mix together tablespoon flour, baking powder, and salt. Mix into eggs. Stir in nuts, coconut, and dates or raisins. Spread over crust. Return to oven for 25 minutes. Cool in pan, then cut into bars.

Yield: 30 bars
Sonya Felipe

COCONUT BROWNIES (MOLASSES COOKIES)

½ cup brown sugar
1 cup vegetable shortening
1 pint molasses

1 pound dry coconut
4 cups flour

Mix ingredients in order named. Sugar, vegetable shortening, and molasses may be mixed by mixer. Add coconut by hand, and then flour to a stiff dough. Put in refrigerator for 6 to 8 hours or overnight. Pinch off small pieces, roll in hand, place on greased cookie sheet. Press flat with fork that has been dipped in milk. Bake in hot oven, 475 degrees, for 6 minutes. Store in sealed container; improve with age.

Note: If dough gets sticky before finishing making them out, return to refrigerator for a short time.

Yield: 100 Brownies
Kay Everngam

CARAMEL RIBBON BROWNIES

24 caramels (7-ounce package)
1 5½-ounce can evaporated milk
1 2-layer chocolate cake mix
1 cup chopped nuts

6 tablespoons butter
½ cup semi-sweet chocolate
   pieces

Cook caramels and 2 tablespoons evaporated milk over low heat until melted. Combine remaining milk, cake mix, nuts and butter. Mix well. Spread half of cake mixture in greased 13x9x2-inch pan. Bake at 350 degrees for 10 minutes. Sprinkle chocolate pieces over hot baked crust. Drizzle caramel mixture by teaspoon over all. Put other half of cake mixture on top and bake 20 minutes more. Cut into bars while warm. Cool in pan.

Yield: 36 bars
Joyce Zeigler

CHERRY FRUIT CHEWS

¼ cup butter or margarine,
   softened
1 cup sugar
2 eggs
1¼ cups biscuit mix

1 cup chopped walnuts
1 cup cut-up dates
1 jar (4-ounce) maraschino
   cherries, drained, chopped

Heat oven to 350 degrees. Mix butter, sugar, and eggs; stir in biscuit mix. Gently fold in nuts, dates, and cherries. Spread dough in greased oblong pan, 13x9x2. Bake 30 minutes. Cool slightly, cut into 1¼ inch squares. To decorate, sprinkle top with red sugar. Moist, rich bars, good travelers, and keep well.

Yield: 4 dozen
Virginia Brown

CRANBERRY APPLE SPICE BARS

1 cup flour
¼ teaspoon salt
¼ cup margarine, melted
½ cup brown sugar
½ cup white sugar
1 egg
1 teaspoon vanilla

¼ cup sour cream
½ cup chopped cranberries
½ cup chopped, pared apples
½ cup chopped walnuts
1 teaspoon baking powder
¼ teaspoon cinnamon

Sift together flour, salt, baking powder, and cinnamon. Cream margarine, sugars, and egg. Add vanilla and sour cream. Stir in sifted ingredients, then cranberries, apples, and nuts. Sprinkle topping on before baking. Bake in greased 8x8x2-inch pan at 350 degrees for 30 minutes. Cool before cutting.

TOPPING

1 tablespoon sugar

½ teaspoon cinnamon

Yield: 16 bars
Beth Adams

DATE NUT PIN WHEELS

2¼ cups chopped dates
1 cup sugar
1 cup water
1 cup nuts
2 cups brown sugar

1 cup shortening
3 eggs
½ teaspoon salt
½ teaspoon soda
4 cups flour

Mix dates, sugar, water, and nuts. Cook for 5 minutes. Cool. Cream shortening with brown sugar. Add eggs and flour, soda, and salt. Mix well and roll thin into a rectangle, using more flour if necessary. Spread with date mixture and roll up like a jelly roll. Wrap in waxed paper and refrigerate overnight. Slice thin. Bake for 15 minutes at 375 degrees.

Yield: 5 dozen
Martha Short

OLD CAROLINE COUNTY DROP COOKIES

1 cup flour
1 stick butter or margarine
¼ cup brown sugar
¼ cup white sugar
1 egg

¼ cup nuts
¼ cup raisins
½ teaspoon soda
1 tablespoon milk or cream

Cream butter or margarine with brown and white sugars. Add eggs, nuts, raisins, soda, flour, and milk or cream. Bake at 375 degrees for 10 minutes.

Yield: 2½ dozen
Florence F. Nuttle

AUNT HATTIE STORY'S FILLED COOKIES

1 cup sugar
½ cup shortening
1 egg
½ cup milk

3½ cups flour
2 teaspoons cream of tartar
1 teaspoon baking soda
1 teaspoon vanilla

Mix all ingredients. Roll very thin, cut in circles of desired size. Place on greased cookie sheet. Put 1 teaspoon of filling in center of each circle—leave slight rim around filling. Moisten rim with milk. Place another circle on top. Press edges together with fork. Prick top to allow steam to escape. Bake at 350 degrees until brown.

Filling:
1½ cups chopped raisins
⅔ cup sugar

⅔ cup water
2 teaspoons flour

Cook until thick. Be careful not to allow it to burn.

Yield: 4 dozen
Beth Adams

FATTIGMAN

6 egg yolks
¼ cup sugar
1 tablespoon butter (melted)
⅓ cup whipping cream

2 cups sifted flour
1 teaspoon ground cardamom
½ teaspoon salt

Beat egg yolks until thick and lemon colored. Gradually beat in sugar. Gently stir in butter, whip cream until soft peaks form. Fold into egg mixture. Sift together flour, cardamom and salt. Gradually fold just enough flour into yolk mixture to make a soft dough. Chill well.

Divide dough in half. On lightly floured surface, roll each half to an ⅛-inch thickness. Cut dough into 2-inch wide strips, then slash diagonally at 3-inch lengths to make diamonds. Cut slit in center of each diamond and pull one end through. Fry a few at a time in deep hot fat (375 degrees) for 1-1½ minutes, until very light golden brown. Drain on paper towels. While warm, sift a little confectioners sugar over cookies.

Yield: 5 dozen
Janice Trice

MOTHER WHITING'S HERMITS

½ cup sour milk (stir in 1
   teaspoon soda)
1½ cups brown sugar
2 eggs
½ cup shortening
2 teaspoons cinnamon

⅛ teaspoon nutmeg
½ cup molasses
3 cups flour
½ cup raisins
⅛ teaspoon cloves

Melt shortening. Mix sugar and molasses. Add well beaten eggs, sour milk and soda. Add dry ingredients, then melted shortening. Lastly add raisins. Spread then in large, well greased cookie tin (not cookie sheet). Bake at 375 degrees until top appears puffed and shiny. Makes a large batch. Carries well for picnics, boat trips, etc. and keeps well if stored in a covered tin.

Yield: 6 dozen
Gladys Whiting

KRUMKAKE

3 eggs
½ cup sugar
½ cup cold water

½ cup cooled, melted butter
½ teaspoon vanilla
1 cup flour

Beat eggs with sugar until light. Add cold water, butter, vanilla and flour. Stir until smooth. Heat Krumkake iron over low heat. Brush lightly with melted butter. Pour about 1 tablespoon batter into iron. Cook wafer slowly until golden on one side, turn and cook on the other side. Remove each wafer with a fork and roll over cylinder. May be sprinkled with powdered sugar or filled with fruit, or fruit and whipped cream.

Yield: 5 dozen
Sonya Felipe

INDOOR S'MORES

⅔ cup light corn syrup
2 tablespoons butter or margarine
1 12-ounce package chocolate morsels

1 teaspoon vanilla
1 package (10-ounce) grahams cereal (about 8 cups)
3 cups miniature marshmallows

Butter baking pan, 13x9x2-inches. Heat corn syrup, margarine, and chocolate morsels just to boiling in 3-quart saucepan, stirring constantly; remove from heat. Stir in vanilla. Pour over cereal in large mixing bowl. Toss quickly until completely coated with chocolate. Fold in marshmallows, 1 cup at a time. Press mixture evenly in pan with buttered back of spoon. Let stand until firm, at least 1 hour. Cut into about 1½-inch squares.

Yield: 48 squares
Ida M. Gordon

ICE BOX COOKIES

2 cups sugar
1 cup shortening
1 cup clabber (sour milk)
1 teaspoon baking soda

1 teaspoon baking powder
Flavoring
2½ to 3 cups flour, or enough
   to roll thin

Cream sugar and shortening. Add dry ingredients alternately with milk. Stir in flavoring. Put in "ice-box" overnight. Roll very thin. Cut into desired shapes. Bake at 350 degrees 6 to 5 minutes.

Yield: 4 to 5 dozen
Mrs. Wilbert Callaway

CHOICE MERINGUES

2 egg whites
⅔ cup sugar
¼ teaspoon vanilla
Pinch of salt
¼ teaspoon cream of tartar

Package of small chocolate
   chips or shave ½ square
   of chocolate
¼ cup finely chopped nuts

Beat egg whites stiff. Add sugar, vanilla, salt, and cream of tartar. Stir in chocolate and nuts. Put foil on cookie sheet. Push 1 teaspoon of meringue off with knife 8 rows of six meringues. Put meringues in preheated 350 degree oven. Close door. Turn off heat. Do not open until morning, or six hours, or they may be placed in 250 degree oven for 50 minutes instead.

Yield: 48 meringues
Florence F. Nuttle

LEMON KRUMKAKE

3 eggs well beaten
½ cup sugar
½ cup butter

½ cup flour
1 teaspoon lemon extract

Beat eggs with sugar until light. Add butter, lemon extract and flour. Stir until smooth. Heat Krumkake iron over low heat, brush lightly with melted butter. Pour about 1 tablespoon batter into iron. Cook wafer slowly until golden on one side, turn and cook on the other side. Remove each wafer with a fork and roll over cylinder. May be sprinkled with powdered sugar or filled with fruit, or fruit and whipped cream.

Yield: 5 dozen
Sonya Felipe

LACE COOKIES

1 cup flour
1 cup chopped, flaked coconut or
  chopped nuts
1½ cups light corn syrup

½ cup firmly packed brown
  sugar
½ cup margarine
1 teaspoon vanilla

Mix together. Bring to boil over medium heat, stirring constantly. Drop by scant teaspoon onto foil covered cookie sheet, 3 inches apart. Bake at 350 degrees for 8 to 10 minutes. Cool 3 or 4 minutes until foil can be peeled off. Place cookies on absorbent paper.

Yield: 4 dozen
Mrs. Florence M. Howard

AUNT KATE KING ZEIGLER'S PENNY CAKES

3 pounds sugar
1 pound lard
Salt
1 quart buttermilk

3 teaspoons soda
2 teaspoons cream of tartar
Flour enough to roll

Mix together. Chill over night and roll and bake.

Yield: 20 to 24 dozen

The above is original recipe Circa 1904. Present recipe is as follows:

2 cups sugar
¾ cup shortening
1 teaspoon salt
1 teaspoon soda

¾ teaspoon cream of tartar
1 cup buttermilk
1 teaspoon vanilla
Flour enough to roll

Note: In the early part of the century, these cookies were made by "Aunt Kate" and sold to berry pickers near Denton, Maryland, for one penny each.

Yield: 4 to 5 dozen
Joyce Zeigler

BRILLIANT CANDY SLICES

1 cup butter
1 cup sifted powdered sugar
1 unbeaten egg
1 teaspoon vanilla

2¼ cups sifted flour
1 cup pecans
2 cups soft candied cherries
    (green and red) cut in half

Cream butter, add powdered sugar. Blend in egg and vanilla. Add sifted flour and mix well. Stir in pecans and candied cherries. Chill 1 hour. Divide in thirds. Shape into rolls 10 inches long. Wrap in waxed paper. Chill 3 hours. Cut into thin slices, place on ungreased sheet and bake at 325 degrees for 12 to 15 minutes.

Yield: 100 to 120 slices
Jean W. Dwyer

SOFT MOLASSES COOKIES

1 egg beaten
1 cup molasses
½ cup shortening (scant)
1 teaspoon ginger

4 cups flour
Pinch of salt
1 teaspoon soda (dissolved in
   1 tablespoon vinegar)

Add molasses to egg. Add shortening, salt, ginger, and beat. Add four and soda. Add about ½ cup more flour or enough to make dough to roll. Roll ⅓ inch thick. Cut, bake on greased sheet at 350 degrees until light brown.

Yield: 2½ dozen
Beth Adams

MOLASSES DROP COOKIES

12 ounces molasses
1 pound brown sugar
2 eggs
1½ cups vegetable shortening
1 cup water
2 tablespoons baking soda in
   water

½ teaspoon salt
Flour enough to stiffen mixture
   for dropping from spoon
½ teaspoon ginger (if desired)

Beat together brown sugar, eggs, and vegetable shortening. Add molasses and salt to mix. Put soda in water and add to mixture.

Sift into the mixture enough flour to stiffen. Add ginger to flour if desired. Drop by tablespoon on cookie sheet. Brush top with beaten egg and bake at 350 degrees for 10 to 15 minutes.

Yield: 4 dozen
Mrs. Robert Graham

OLD FASHIONED APPLE CRISP

4 cups peeled apples sliced (about
    5 medium apples)
¼ cup brown sugar

1 tablespoon all-purpose flour
2 teaspoons lemon juice

In 8-inch square baking dish or shallow 1½ quart casserole, combine apples, brown sugar, flour and lemon juice. Mix well.

TOPPING

1 cup quick or old fashioned
    oats (uncooked)
¼ cup all purpose flour
¼ cup packed brown sugar

¼ teaspoon salt
¼ teaspoon ground cinnamon
⅓ cup butter or margarine
    (melted)

Heat oven to 375 degrees. Combine oats, ¼ cup flour, ¼ cup brown sugar, salt, and cinnamon; mix well. Add butter, mix well until crumbly. Sprinkle over apple mix. Bake about 30 minutes or until apples are tender and topping is golden brown. Serve with sweetened whipped cream or ice cream, if desired.

Yield: 6 servings
Betty Fleetwood

YANKEE DOODLE APPLE DESSERT

½ cup sifted cake flour
¾ cup firmly packed light brown
    sugar
1 teaspoon baking powder
¼ teaspoon salt
Dash of mace

Dash of cinnamon
1 egg
½ teaspoon vanilla
1 cup chopped tart apples
½ cup chopped walnuts

Mix and sift first 6 ingredients. Stir in unbeaten egg and vanilla. Fold in apples and walnuts. Turn into well-greased 8-inch pie pan. Bake at 350 degrees for 25 to 30 minutes or until brown and crusty. Garnish with whipped cream sprinkled with cinnamon or scoops of vanilla ice cream.

Yield: 1 8-inch pie
Carter M. Hickman

APPLE BUTTER CUSTARD

1½ cups spicy apple butter
¾ cup light brown sugar,
   firmly packed

2 large eggs, beaten
2 cups rich milk or cream

Use any custard or pumpkin recipe and add apple butter instead of pumpkin. Add brown sugar, eggs beaten and milk or cream to thick apple butter. Bake in large pan, in hot oven, 15 minutes at 425 degrees. Then set dial for 350 degrees for 30 minutes or until an inserted knife comes out clean. You can add strips of dough across top of pie if you like.

Yield: 1 pie
Alda Pearson

APPLE KUCHEN

2 cups flour
2 teaspoons baking powder
½ teaspoon salt
6 tablespoons margarine
¾ cup sugar
2 eggs

½ cup milk
1 teaspoon vanilla
1 teaspoon cinnamon
¼ cup sugar
6 to 8 tart apples

Peel and core apples. Slice into 8ths. Cream margarine; add sugar and mix until fluffy. Add eggs and vanilla and blend well. Sift together flour, salt, and baking powder. Add alternately to sugar-margarine-egg mixture, with the milk. Spread batter in a 15x10-inch jelly roll pan. Arrange apple slices on top of batter, close together. Combine sugar and cinnamon and sprinkle over apple slices. Bake in 370 degree oven for 35 minutes.

Yield: 16 to 20 servings
Regina Mueller

NEVER FAIL BAKED CUSTARD

4 cups scalded milk
½ cup sugar

4 eggs beaten slightly
¼ teaspoon salt

Mix ingredients together and fill small or large containers. Place containers in pan of hot water. Sprinkle grated nutmeg on top of custards. Bake at 375 degrees for 30 minutes.

Yield: 8 servings
Florence F. Nuttle

BREAD PUDDING
(low cholesterol)

4½ cups dry bread crumbs
   (11 slices)
3 cups scalded milk
2 beaten eggs (or 1 package
   instant imitation eggs)

1 cup sugar
¼ teaspoon salt
¼ teaspoon cinnamon
1 teaspoon vanilla
½ cup raisins, if desired

Mix thoroughly. Pour into *greased* baking dish and set in pan of hot water. Bake in 350 degree oven one hour. Serve warm or cold.

Yield: 8 servings
Laura Rogers

"DIET" BREAD PUDDING

1 slice bread, plain or raisin
1 cup skim milk
1 egg
1 teaspoon vanilla

2 individual packages sugar
   substitute
Dash ground cinnamon
Grating of nutmeg

Break bread in small pieces in 1-quart casserole. Beat egg in small bowl, add milk and seasonings. Mix well. Pour over bread. Place casserole in pan of water and bake 30 to 40 minutes in 350 degree oven, or until custard is firm.

Yield: 1 serving
Janice Trice

MINIATURE CHEESE CAKES

2 8-ounce packages of cream
   cheese—softened
2 eggs
2 teaspoons vanilla

¾ cup sugar
1 can cherry pie filling
Crushed vanilla wafers or
   graham cracker crumbs

Mix first 4 ingredients for 5 minutes at medium speed. Use small tart or miniature muffin tins lined with paper petit four cups. Place crushed vanilla wafer in each paper. Fill with cream mixture. Bake at 350 degrees for 12 minutes. Top with pie filling.

Yield: Approximately 60 tarts
Sonya Felipe

NORA ROBERTS' BREAD PUDDING

5 slices bread torn into pieces
   (4-6 pieces per slice)
3-4 eggs (depending on size),
   lightly beaten
1 cup sugar
Pinch salt
Cinnamon to taste—
   approximately 1½-2
   tablespoons

3½ cups milk
½ stick margarine, melted
1 teaspoon vanilla
1 pound raisins (or less)

Mix everything together in a 2-2½ quart casserole. Cook uncovered at 350 degrees for one hour. Bread pudding can be eaten plain, in a dish with milk, or any other way you want.

Yield: 8 servings
Nora Roberts, Author for
Silhouette Romances

OLD FASHIONED CHERRY PUDDING

½ cup sugar
¼ cup butter
1 egg
½ cup milk

1¼ cups flour
Pinch salt
2 teaspoons baking powder
1 cup pitted sour cherries

Cream sugar and butter. Add milk, egg, flour, salt and baking powder. Dust cherries with flour so they won't sink. Fold in last. Bake and serve. Bake at 350 degrees for 35 to 40 minutes.

Yield: 4 to 6 servings
Ann King Nies
From King Clan Cook Book

CRACKER PUDDING

1 quart milk
1¼ cups cracker crumbs
½ cup coconut
Yolks of 2 eggs

2 beaten egg whites
Scant cup sugar
1½ teaspoons vanilla

Heat milk, add cracker crumbs, coconut, egg yolks and sugar. Cook in double boiler. Beat egg whites stiff. Either fold beaten egg whites into mixture or spread over top and brown in oven.

Yield: 6 to 8 servings
From kitchen of Aunt Mary Habacker
Courtesy of King Clan Cook Book

CHERRY DELIGHT

First Layer
1 cup flour   ½ cup pecans (chopped)
½ cup melted butter

Mix and pat into 9x13-inch pan. Bake at 350 degrees for 15 minutes. Let cool.

Second Layer
8 ounces softened cream cheese   1 cup whipped topping
1 cup powdered sugar

Blend. Fold in whipped topping. Spread over layer 1 and chill 15 to 30 minutes.

Third Layer

Spread 1 can cherry pie filling.

Fourth Layer
2 packages instant vanilla   1 teaspoon vanilla
    pudding   3 cups milk

Mix and spread over cherry and chill.

Fifth Layer

Spread with whipped topping and sprinkle with pecans.

Yield: 16 servings
Barbara Quinn

CHESAPEAKE TORTE

1 egg	⅛ teaspoon salt
¾ cup sugar	½ cup chopped nutmeats
2 tablespoons flour	½ cup chopped apples
1¼ teaspoons baking powder	1 teaspoon vanilla

Beat eggs and sugar together until very smooth. Combine flour, baking powder, and salt. Stir into egg mixture. Add nutmeats, apples, and vanilla. Bake in greased pie pan in moderate oven (350 degrees) 35 minutes. Top with whipped cream or ice cream.

Yield: 4 servings
Carol Stockley

STEAMED CHOCOLATE PUDDING

1 cup flour	1 egg
½ cup sugar	1 teaspoon butter
½ cup milk	1 teaspoon baking powder
1 square chocolate	

Mix sugar and beaten egg, milk and flour sifted with the baking powder and salt. Add melted chocolate and butter. Fill pudding mold, cover and steam 2 hours. Serve with sauce.

SAUCE

2 eggs	1 tablespoon butter
1 cup sugar	2 tablespoons hot milk

Beat eggs and sugar together until light. Add butter and hot milk. Beat until well blended.

Yield: 8 to 16 slices
Beth Adams

FRUIT COMPOTE

1 pound pitted prunes
½ of an 11-ounce package
    apricots
1 (13-ounce) can pineapple
    chunks with juice

1 pound can cherry pie filling
2 cups water
¼ cup sherry

Place prunes in 9-inch square baking dish Top with apricots and pineapple chunks. Combine cherry pie filling and water and sherry. Pour over fruits. Bake at 350 degrees for 1½ hours. Serve warm.

Yield: 8 to 10 servings
Kay Everngam

DEEP DISH FRUIT DELIGHT

Crust:
1 cup flour
1 teaspoon baking powder
¾ cup water
1 egg

2 tablespoons sugar
½ teaspoon salt
⅔ cup solid vegetable shortening

Blend crust ingredients at low speed for ½ minute. Beat 2 minutes at medium speed. Spread batter in baking dish (8x12-inch)

Filling:
3 cups fruit (blueberries,
    cherries, strawberries)
3 tablespoons cornstarch

½ cup water
1 cup sugar

Cook 1 cup fruit with rest of filling ingredients until thickened. Fold in remaining berries. Spoon filling evenly in middle of crust batter. Bake at 400 degrees for 35 to 40 minutes until golden brown.

Yield: 8 servings
Barbara Quinn

LEMON CUPS

2 tablespoons soft butter	4 tablespoons flour
1 cup sugar	1/8 teaspoon salt (pinch)
5 tablespoons lemon juice	3 eggs (separated)
Rind of 1 lemon (grated)	1½ cups milk

Preheat oven to 350 degrees. In large bowl cream sugar and butter. Add flour, salt, lemon juice, and lemon rind. Beat egg yolks, add milk, stir well. Pour egg yolks and milk into first mixture, stir well. Beat egg whites until stiff and fold into batter. Mixture will be very thin. Fill custard cups full to top. Set cups about half deep in baking pan of hot water. Bake 40 to 45 minutes in oven. When done, you have delicious sponge cake on top and delicious lemon custard on bottom.

Yield: 6 large cups or 7 to 8 small cups
Governor Harry R. Hughes
State of Maryland
Annapolis, Md.

HEAVENLY DESSERT

4 egg whites	1 pint whipping cream
1 cup sugar	2 cups colored miniature
40 butter crackers rolled fine	marshmallows
1 cup chopped nuts	Coconut

Beat egg whites until stiff, gradually add sugar (1 tablespoon at a time), beating well after each addition. When stiff fold in crackers and nuts. Pour into a buttered 9x13-inch pan. Bake 20 to 30 minutes at 350 degrees until light golden around edge. Cool.

Topping: Whip whipping cream until stiff. Add marshmallows. Spread over cooled mixture and sprinkle flaked coconut over top. Refrigerate 24 hours.

Yield: 15 servings
Hazel Carey

MY BEST GINGERBREAD

½ cup sugar
½ cup butter
1 egg
3 or 4 tablespoons molasses,
    adding enough light or dark
    syrup to make a cup

2½ cups sifted flour
1½ teaspoons soda
½ teaspoon ginger
1 teaspoon cinnamon
½ teaspoon cloves
½ teaspoon salt

Cream sugar, butter, egg and molasses mix. Add dry ingredients. Add 1 cup hot water and beat until smooth. Batter will be quite thin. Bake in moderate oven (350 degrees).

Yield: 12 servings
Vera Van Shaick

NESSELRODE PUDDING MOLD

4 eggs, separated
1 can (13 ounce) evaporated
    skim milk
1 cup water
2 envelopes unflavored gelatin
¼ teaspoon salt
2 teaspoons vanilla

1 teaspoon brandy or rum
    flavoring
3 tablespoons chopped nuts
5 tablespoons raisins
5 chopped maraschino cherries
5 tablespoons sugar or sugar
    substitute

Beat egg yolks slightly, just to mix, in heavy sauce pan. Stir in evaporated milk, water, gelatin and salt. Cook over medium low heat until mixture is slightly thickened and coats a metal spoon. Stir in vanilla and brandy flavoring. Pour mixture into a bowl. Place bowl over another bowl filled with ice water. Chill, stirring frequently until mixture mounds slightly when dropped from a spoon. Fold in nuts, raisins and cherries.

    Beat egg whites until foamy, fold in sugar. Beat until stiff. Fold in gelatin mixture. Turn into a 6 cup mold. Refrigerate 3 hours or until firm. Unmold and garnish with maraschino cherries.

Yield: 8 servings at 159 calories each
Marinanne Kent

LOW CALORIE PINEAPPLE MOUSSE
45 calories per serving

1 teaspoon unflavored gelatin
¾ cup unsweetened crushed
   pineapple
½ cup unsweetened pineapple
   juice
½ cup low calorie whipped cream

1 teaspoon lemon juice
¼ teaspoon granular sugar
   substitute
2 tablespoons cold water
Pinch of salt

Soften gelatin in 2 tablespoons water. Add sweetener to pineapple juice and bring to a boil. Stir in gelatin. Mix well. Remove from heat, add salt and let cool. Add pineapple and lemon juice and chill until mixture thickens. Fold whipped cream into pineapple mixture. Pour into freezer tray and freeze until firm.

LOW CALORIE WHIPPED CREAM

½ cup non-fat dry powdered milk
¼ teaspoon vanilla
1 teaspoon lemon juice

1 teaspoon granular sugar
   substitute
½ cup ice cold water

Place water in mixing bowl. Add remaining ingredients and beat until stiff.

Yield: 4 servings
Sara Kidd

HOLIDAY PLUM PUDDING

1 cup chopped beef suet
1 cup molasses
1 cup sweet milk
2 small teaspoons soda
1 teaspoon salt

3 cups flour
½ teaspoon cinnamon
¼ teaspoon cloves
¼ teaspoon allspice
1 cup raisins or chopped dates

Steam in mold for 3 hours. Invert on rack to cool. May be frozen and reheated in mold before serving. Top slices with hard sauce or whipped cream.

Yield: 1 large pudding
Beth Adams

RICE PUDDING WITHOUT EGGS

2 quarts milk
1½ cups raw rice
½ teaspoon salt

1 cup sugar
Dash of ground cinnamon, or
  freshly grated nutmeg

Wash rice carefully. Mix rice with salt, sugar, spice, and milk. Place in a three-quart casserole, cover and bake 2½ to 3 hours in a 275 degree oven. Stir occasionally. The grains of rice should be large and whole and the milk creamy.

Yield: 8 to 10 servings
Mrs. Walter Avery Johnson, Sr.

BAKED RICE PUDDING

¼ cup raw short grain rice
6 tablespoons sugar
½ teaspoon salt

1 tablespoon butter
1 quart milk
Nutmeg grated over the top

Combine all ingredients in a greased 1½-quart casserole. Bake at 325 degrees for 2½ hours. After one hour stir. Be sure to loosen any crust that has formed on the sides of casserole. Stir down crust at half hour intervals.

Yield: 1½ quarts
Regina Mueller

STRAWBERRY WHIP
(Eastern Shore)

2 stiffly beaten egg whites
1 cup sugar

1 cup berries, mashed

Use in place of whipped cream on strawberry shortcake.

Ann Clark

WALNUT TORTE

6 egg yolks
1 cup sugar
1 teaspoon vanilla
½ cup sifted flour
½ pound ground nuts, finely
    ground

6 stiffly beaten egg whites
1 teaspoon melted butter
1 teaspoon baking powder

Beat egg yolks for 5 minutes. Add sugar. Beat 5 minutes. Add vanilla and butter. Fold in alternately ground nuts and stiffly beaten egg whites. Bake in greased 9-inch layer cake pans. Cover bottom of pan with waxed paper. Bake at 350 degrees for 25 minutes. Let cool. Cover whole cake with whipped cream.

Yield: 12-14 servings
Mrs. Peter R. Derringer

PO' MAN'S CHAIN SAW MASSACRE PUDDING

1 loaf day-old bread
1 quart milk
3 eggs, beaten
4 tablespoons butter, melted
1 cup raisins
1 cup chopped, pitted prunes
2 ounces dark rum

1 cup chopped apples
1½ cups brown sugar
½ teaspoon salt
½ teaspoon cinnamon
3 teaspoons vanilla or almond
    flavoring
½ cup chopped nuts (optional)

Tear bread into small pieces in large bowl. Add beaten eggs and all other ingredients; mix with slotted spoon. Turn into buttered 3-quart deep casserole. Bake for about one hour at 350 degrees. When firm, take to the table warm, and "massacre" with a large knife and serving spoon. Serve in individual bowls. Top with whipped cream if desired.

Yield: 12 to 15 servings
Max Chambers

VIENNESE CHRISTY TORTE

1 cup semi-sweet chocolate
   chips, melted
4 egg yolks
½ cup butter, softened

2 teaspoons confectioners sugar
¼ cup water (warm)
1 teaspoon vanilla
1 pound cake (1 pound)

Blend all ingredients in a blender. Chill. Slice cake in three layers. Frost each layer with chilled mixture and chill again. Slice thin, extremely rich.

Yield: 12 servings
Christie Huffman

RHUBARB TARTS

1½ cups chopped rhubarb
1 cup sugar
4 tablespoons flour

3 tablespoons fruit juice (orange,
   pineapple, or apple)
2 eggs

Make and bake 6 pastry shells—cool.
   Cook rhubarb, sugar, flour, and juice until rhubarb is tender. Add 2 beaten eggs and cook until thickened and smooth. Cool. Fill shells just before serving. Top with whipped cream and add a whole strawberry.

Yield: 6 tarts
Beth Adams

PUDDING SAUCE SUPREME

3 tablespoons boiling water
1 cup powdered sugar
2 egg yolks, beaten
½ cup vegetable shortening

1 tablespoon butter
1 teaspoon flavoring
1 cup heavy cream, whipped

Add boiling water to sugar and stir until completely dissolved. Add beaten egg yolks. Place over hot water and heat thoroughly. stirring constantly. Melt vegetable shortening and butter together and add to sugar mixture. Cool. Add flavoring. (Try vanilla with lemon). Fold in whipped cream.

Yield: 2 cups
Mrs. Helene Thawley

WEBSTER'S DELIGHT

#1

1 package Holland Rusks, rolled
   fine

½ cup melted butter
½ cup sugar

#2

2 cups milk
½ cup sugar
3 egg yolks

2 tablespoons cornstarch
Salt and vanilla to taste

Cook #2 ingredients in double boiler stirring constantly until thick.

#3

Beat whites of eggs and add 3 tablespoons sugar

Butter pan well. Put in ½ of #1, then put in all of #2 on top. Put all of #3 on top of that. Put balance of #1 on top of that. Bake 30 minutes in moderate oven (355 degrees). Let cool. Cut in squares and serve with whipped cream.

Yield: 10 to 12 servings
Kay Everngam

APPLE COBBLER OR PEACH COBBLER

1 cup whole wheat flour
1 tablespoon sugar
¼ teaspoon salt
1½ teaspoons baking powder

¼ cup butter or margarine
1 egg beaten, plus enough milk
   to make 1 cup
Apples or peaches

Peel and slice fruit to fill one inch in an 8x8-inch pyrex dish. Sprinkle with cinnamon. Sift dry ingredients together into a bowl. Blend in shortening. Add milk and egg combination to dry ingredients. Stir to blend. Spread over prepared fruit and bake at 400 degrees for 40 minutes.

Yield: 8 servings
Regina Mueller

PERFECT PIE CRUST

1½ cups flour
1 tablespoon cornstarch
⅛ teaspoon cream of tartar

⅓ teaspoon salt
½ cup shortening
¼ cup cold water

Sift flour, cornstarch, cream of tartar, and salt. Cut in shortening. Add water, mixing lightly. Roll out on floured board.

Yield: two 9-inch pie crust shells
Pauline Myers

FOOLPROOF PIE CRUST

4 cups flour
1 tablespoon sugar
1¾ cups vegetable shortening
2 teaspoons salt

1 egg
½ cup water
1 tablespoon vinegar

Blend first four ingredients with fork or hand blender. Beat egg, vinegar and water. Combine the two mixtures, stirring with fork until all ingredients are moistened. Mold dough with hands. Divide into 5 balls, wrap each in plastic wrap. Put in refrigerator or freezer before using. Makes 5 crusts. Save any trimmings and put in plastic in freezer until another crust is formed. May be handled as much as you like. Rolls out very easily.

Note: If mixture seems dry, let it rest for a few minutes before molding.

Yield: 5 crusts
Kay Everngam

LEMON MERINGUE PIE

½ cup water
7 tablespoons cornstarch
1½ cups water
1¼ cups sugar

3 egg yolks, slightly beaten
1 lemon (grated rind and juice)
1 tablespoon butter
1 baked pie shell

Mix ½ cup water and cornstarch to thin paste. Combine 1½ cups water and sugar in top of double boiler and bring to boil over direct heat. Add cornstarch paste and cook until mixture begins to thicken; return to double boiler and continue cooking until thick and smooth (15 minutes). Pour over slightly beaten egg yolks, return to double boiler, and cook 1 minute longer. Add lemon rind and juice, and butter and blend well. Cool and pour into pie shell. Top with meringue.

Meringue:
3 egg whites
9 tablespoons sugar

1 teaspoon lemon juice

Beat egg whites until stiff but not dry. Add sugar gradually, beating constantly. Add lemon juice. Pile lightly on filling in baked pie shell. Bake in slow oven (325 degrees) 15 minutes, or until firm and delicately browned.

Crust:
1¼ cups sifted flour
½ teaspoon salt

⅓ cup vegetable shortening
3 tablespoons water

Sift flour and salt together. Add ½ shortening to flour. Cut in with pastry blender or 2 knives until mixture looks like meal. Add remaining shortening and continue cutting until particles are size of navy beans. Sprinkle water, 1 tablespoon at a time, over mixture. With fork work lightly together until all particles are moistened and in lumps. Add just enough water to moisten. Press dampened particles together into a ball. Do not handle dough any more than necessary.

Yield: 1 pie
Helene Thawley

CHOCOLATE MINT PIE

1 cup milk
32 marshmallows
Pinch of salt
½ teaspoon peppermint extract
Green food coloring
1 pint whipping cream
Crushed chocolate wafers (about
    11 ounces)

Chocolate Sauce:
1 cup corn syrup
2 squares chocolate
½ teaspoon vanilla

Heat milk in double boiler. Add marshmallows. Stir until melted. Add salt, peppermint extract, and a few drops green food coloring. Cool and fold in whipped cream.

Crush chocolate wafers and line pie dish. Pour mint mixture into pie shell and chill for several hours.

Heat syrup and chocolate until chocolate is melted. Add vanilla. Cool and serve over pie.

Yield: 1 pie
Hettie Russell

MOUNTAIN PIE

½ stick butter
1 cup sugar
Pinch salt
1 cup flour

1½ teaspoons baking powder
¾ cup milk
2 cups fruit mixed with ¼ cup
    sugar

Mix first six items together. Put all ingredients except fruit into lightly greased baking pan. Pour fruit into center. Bake in 350 degree oven until fruit appears dry on top. Serve like pie or pudding. Can be topped with favorite sauce or whipped cream.

Yield: 1 pie
Emily Pindell

CHOCOLATE LAYER PIE

First Layer:
1½ cups flour
1½ sticks oleo melted

½ cup chopped pecans

Mix and spread in a 9x13-inch pan. Bake at 315 degrees for 20 minutes. Cool.

Second Layer:
8 ounces cream cheese
1 cup of powdered sugar

1 cup of whipped topping
(large bowl)

Mix and spread over first layer

Third Layer:
2 packages small instant
    chocolate pudding

3 cups milk

Mix for 2 minutes on low speed. Spread over second layer.

Fourth Layer:

Spread remaining whipped topping. Sprinkle with nuts. Refrigerate.

Yield: 1 pie
Jean W. Dwyer.

PECAN TASSIES

3 ounces soft cream cheese
½ cup butter
1 cup flour
⅔ cup coarsely broken pecans
    or walnuts

1 egg
⅔ cup brown sugar
1 tablespoon butter
1 teaspoon vanilla
Dash of salt

Blend together cream cheese, ½ cup butter, and flour. Chill about 1 hour. Shape into 24 1-inch balls. Press dough against small muffin pan. Sprinkle with nuts. Beat together egg, brown sugar, 1 tablespoon butter, vanilla, and salt until smooth. Pour egg mixture over nuts. Bake in preheated 325 degree oven for 25 minutes or until filling is set. Cool thoroughly before removing from pan.

Yield: 24 tassies
Marianne Kent

PECAN PIE

½ cup white corn syrup
½ cup brown sugar
3 eggs beaten
Lump of butter melted (4
    tablespoons)

½ teaspoon vanilla
1 cup pecans, chopped
1 unbaked pie shell

Mix sugar and syrup. Add butter, eggs, vanilla, and nuts. Pour into un-baked pie shell. Bake about 50 minutes in slow oven (325 degrees).

Yield: 1 pie
Pauline Myers

PECAN PIE

¼ cup butter
⅔ cup brown sugar (firmly
    packed)
¼ teaspoon salt

¾ cup dark corn syrup
3 eggs, beaten
1 teaspoon vanilla
1 cup pecans

Cream butter and sugar together until fluffy. Add the other 4 ingre-dients. Line pan with pastry. Add filling and sprinkle with pecans. Bake at 450 degrees for 10 minutes. Reduce temperature to 350 degrees and bake for 35 minutes. Pie is done when knife comes out clean when in-serted.

Yield: 1 pie
Caroline L. Wheatley

PEACH COBBLER

8 or 10 peaches
1 teaspoon cinnamon
½ cup butter

½ cup sugar
½ cup brown sugar
1 cup flour

Slice enough peaches to fill 1-quart baking dish almost to the top. Sprinkle with cinnamon.

Cut butter into flour, add sugar and stir to form a crumbly mixture. Spread on top of peaches and bake at 350 degrees for 40 minutes. Serve hot or cold.

Yield: 6 to 8 servings
Marianne Kent

NUT PIE

12 graham crackers broken into
    small pieces
1 cup sugar

1 cup broken walnuts
3 egg whites, beaten stiff
1 teaspoon baking powder

Beat sugar and egg whites (I beat egg whites until they begin to stiffen and gradually add sugar). Add remaining ingredients. Mix well. Pour into pie pan (it is best to use a pyrex pan—easier to remove). Press mixture around the pan and sort of pile up around the edges like a crust would be. Bake at 350 degrees for ½ hour. Cool. Put on topping of 1 cup sour cream mixed with 1 teaspoon vanilla and 3½ tablespoons sugar. Put back into the 350 degree oven for 5 minutes. Chill thoroughly before serving.

Yield: 1 9-inch pie
Mrs. Dude Willoughby

FRENCH STRAWBERRY PIE

1 9-inch baked pie shell
1 quart strawberries (plus ½
   cup to slice)
1 cup sugar

3 tablespoons cornstarch
1 3-ounce package cream
   cheese
1 cup whipping cream

Mash berries (reserve 10 to 12 for decoration). Bring mashed berries to a boil; add sugar and cornstarch; cook until thick. Cool.

Whip cream, add 2 tablespoons to cream cheese, beat until smooth and spread in baked pie shell. Put a few sliced berries on cream cheese.

Pour cold thickened berries on cheese mix; top with remaining whipped cream. Garnish with reserved whole berries. Refrigerate 24 hours.

Yield: 6 to 8 servings
Kay Everngam

GLAZED STRAWBERRY PIE

1 9-inch baked pie shell—cooled
2 quarts strawberries
½ cup sugar

3 tablespoons cornstarch
Pinch of salt

Wash, cap and sort berries. Save 1 quart of the largest, ripest berries to fill the pie shell. Mash the other quart and blend in sugar, cornstarch and salt. Heat over low heat stirring constantly until thick and transparent. Cool to just above room temperature. Fill pie shell with reserved whole berries and pour warm glaze over, being sure to cover all the berries. If sauce seems a bit thick, you may add a teaspoon or two of lemon juice to thin it. If sauce is pale you may add a few drops of red food coloring. Chill pie for an hour. Serve with whipped cream or sour cream or whipped topping.

Yield: 1 pie
Sara Kidd

217

SWEET POTATO PIE

2 cups prepared potato
½ cup sugar
2 eggs
1 tablespoon flour
1 cup milk

½ teaspoon each of cinnamon
    and ginger
¼ teaspoon salt
Pastry

Beat eggs and add the sugar, then the potato, salt, and spices. After that, add the flour, and lastly add the milk gradually. Line a pie plate with pastry and pour on it the mixture. Bake for 5 minutes in a brisk (about 400 degrees) oven. Reduce heat to 350 degrees and cook slowly until custard is set.

Yield: 1 pie
Mildred B. Butler

WHITE POTATO PIE

2 pounds potatoes—mashed and
    cooled
½ pound butter
1 pound sugar
5 eggs—separated

2½ cups milk
Little nutmeg
1 teaspoon almond flavoring
½ cup brandy, if desired
2 uncooked pie shells

Cream butter and sugar thoroughly. Add beaten egg yolks. Then add the potatoes. Stir in milk, nutmeg, and flavoring. Lastly, stir in beaten egg whites. Pour into two uncooked pie shells and bake in 350 degree oven for 1 hour.

Yield: 2 pies
Mildred James

APRICOT BALLS

1½ cups of dried apricots
    (ground)

2 cups shredded coconut
⅔ cup sweetened condensed milk

Mix well. Shape into small balls. Roll in powdered sugar.

Yield: 4 to 5 dozen
Pearl McAllister

FUDGE

1 large package chocolate chips
2 squares unsweetened chocolate

1 can condensed milk
1 teaspoon vanilla

Melt above in a double boiler. Stir until thick—then pour into greased pan and cut when cool.

Yield: 24 pieces
Edna Andrew

CLAYTON'S RICH FUDGE

4 squares baking chocolate
2 cups sugar
4 tablespoons corn syrup
¼ teaspoon salt
⅔ cup milk

½ package (2-ounces) German
    sweet chocolate
3 tablespoons butter
1 teaspoon vanilla

Butter one 10-inch square cake pan. Set aside. In 2-quart saucepan mix first five ingredients. Cook over medium heat, stirring constantly, until mixture forms firm ball when dropped into cold water. Remove from heat; add butter. Continue stirring until butter is blended well. Add German chocolate, stirring until melted and blended. Add vanilla, stir well. Pour quickly into prepared pan. Let set until it can be cut into squares. Lift squares onto platter to cool.

Yield: 50 squares (1½-inch)
Clayton Brown

FRUIT AND NUT EASTER EGGS

4 pounds confectioners sugar
4 egg whites (unbeaten)
¼ pound butter
1 medium jar maraschino
  cherries (drained and
  chopped)

1½ cups chopped nuts
Pinch of salt
1 pound semi-sweet chocolate

Mix butter, and some sugar, salt, egg whites, cherries, and nuts, and then balance of sugar. It may be necessary to add a little cherry juice but mixture must be very stiff. Mold in egg shapes and cover with melted semi-sweet chocolate. Place on waxed paper and refrigerate to set.

Hettie Russell

"I've been trying to get up and down with you" is what Eastern Shore people say to a friend who has been difficult to locate.

BUTTER CREAM EASTER EGGS

4 pounds confectioners sugar
3 egg whites unbeaten
½ pound butter

1 teaspoon vanilla
2 tablespoons heavy cream
1 pound semi-sweet chocolate

Mix butter, salt, egg whites, and some of the sugar. Add vanilla and cream, then balance of sugar. Work with hands. If too stiff, add a little more cream. Mold into egg shapes the size you prefer and dip in melted chocolate. Refrigerate to set chocolate.

Hettie Russell

BUCKEYES

1½ cups smooth peanut butter
1 teaspoon vanilla
2 tablespoons oil
1 12-ounce package of chocolate
    chips

½ cup soft margarine
1 16-ounce box powdered sugar

Mix peanut butter, margarine, vanilla, and sugar. Roll into 1-inch balls. Put on waxed paper on cookie sheet. Stick toothpicks in and refrigerate for at least ½ hour. Melt chocolate chips and oil. Dip balls at least halfway into chocolate and refrigerate. Can use milk chocolate, mint, butterscotch or semi-sweet chips.

Yield: 4 dozen balls
Lynnette Scanga

CANDY APPLES

8 medium apples (Insert wooden
    stick in stem end)
2 cups sugar
⅔ cup light corn syrup

1 cup water
½ teaspoon cinnamon flavoring
Red coloring

Stir sugar, syrup and water in pan until sugar almost dissolves. Cover. Bring slowly to a boil. Remove cover and boil rapidly without stirring to 300 degrees (candy thermometer). Add flavoring and color to tint syrup bright red. Remove from heat and stir until blended.
Dip apples—work quickly. Place pan over hot water if necessary to keep syrup thin. Place on cookie sheet (greased).

Yield: 8 servings
Hettie Russell

COCOA FUDGE

1 cup cocoa
4 cups white sugar
2 cups milk

3 tablespoons butter
1 teaspoon vanilla
1 cup chopped nuts

Sift cocoa and sugar together; add milk and stir well. Place over fire and bring to boiling point and boil gently until a little dropped in cold water forms a soft ball. Do not stir during the boiling process. Remove from fire, add butter and let cool. Then add vanilla and chopped nuts and beat until creamy. Pour into buttered pan and mark into squares before it hardens.

Yield: 24 pieces
Miss Elizabeth Vickery

DELICIOUS FUDGE

4½ cups sugar
Pinch of salt
2 tablespoons butter
1 large can evaporated milk
12 ounces of chocolate chips

12 ounces of German sweet
    chocolate
1 jar marshmallow creme
    (7-ounce)
1 cup chopped nuts (optional)

Combine sugar, salt, butter, and evaporated milk in pan and bring to a boil. Lower heat and continue to boil for 7 minutes. Pour over chocolate chips, German sweet chocolate and marshmallow creme and stir until chocolate is melted. Add nuts and pour into large buttered dish or pan and let cool, then cut into pieces and let stand until hardened.

Yield: Approximately 5 pounds
Barbara Maske

MARSHMALLOW BUTTER SCOTCH FUDGE

1 6-ounce package chocolate
   chips
1 6-ounce package butterscotch
   flavored morsels
1 cup chopped nuts

12 large marshmallows (cut up
   with scissors)
2 cups sugar
¾ cup evaporated milk
1 tablespoon butter

Combine chocolate and butterscotch pieces and nuts in bowl. Set aside.
Combine marshmallows, sugar, milk and butter in 2 quart heavy
saucepan. Bring to boil over medium heat, stirring constantly. Continue
to boil 6 minutes, stirring to prevent scorching. Remove from heat. Add
first mixture and beat until creamy and candy thickens. Turn at once into lightly buttered 8 inch square pan. When firm, cut into 36 pieces.

Yield: 36
Mrs. Mildred B. Butler

OLD FASHIONED HARD CANDY

3½ cups sugar
1 cup corn syrup
1 cup water

½ teaspoon oil of flavoring
Food colors

Add all ingredients in saucepan and bring to a boil. Let boil until it
reaches hard crack stage on candy thermometer.

   Have slab of marble cold and buttered. Also butter scissors for cutting. Put wax paper out on flat (table) surface with powdered sugar on it.
Remove syrup from stove and add all flavoring and color. Quickly pour
out on cold marble slab. Cut into strips and roll in powdered sugar. Then
cut into bite size pieces.

Ruth Moore

PEANUT BUTTER FUDGE

2 cups sugar
⅔ cup milk
½ pint jar marshmallow creme
1 cup chunk-style peanut butter

1 teaspoon vanilla
1 6-ounce package semi-sweet
   chocolate pieces

Butter sides of heavy 2 quart saucepan. In it combine sugar and milk. Heat and stir over medium heat until sugar dissolves and mixture comes to boiling. Then cook to soft ball stage. Remove from heat. Add remaining ingredients and stir until blended. Pour into buttered 9x9x2 inch pan. Score in squares while warm. Cut when firm.

Yield: 24 squares
Miss Elizabeth Vickery

PEANUT BUTTER FUDGE

½ pound brown sugar
1 pound white sugar
1¼ pounds peanut butter

1 tablespoon vanilla
1 cup milk or water
Lump of butter

Cook sugar and milk (or water) to soft ball. Add peanut butter and butter, and vanilla. Beat until thick. Pour into buttered pan. (8x8-inch).

Yield: 24 pieces
Mrs. Helene Thawley

SUGAR PECANS

¾ cup sugar
1 teaspoon cinnamon
1 teaspoon salt

1 egg white
1 pound pecans

Combine together the sugar, cinnamon, and salt. Beat egg white until stiff. Using fork, dip pecans in egg white until well covered. Roll in the sugar, cinnamon, and salt. Bake in oven at 250 degrees for 40 minutes. Turn every 10 minutes.

Yield: 1 pound nuts
Jean W. Dwyer

SEAFOAM

2 cups brown sugar
½ cup water

1 egg white
Nuts

Boil sugar and water until it hairs. Pour slowly into stiffly beaten white of 1 egg. Beat quite hard. Stir in nuts. Drop on buttered tins.

Yield: 24 pieces
Mrs. Rita Seely

PULL TAFFY

2 cups granulated sugar
¾ cup water
1 teaspoon vinegar

4 tablespoons butter
¼ teaspoon cream of tartar
1½ teaspoons vanilla

Combine sugar, water, vinegar, butter, and cream of tartar. Boil until it spins slowly into string-like pieces in cold water. Add 1½ teaspoons vanilla. Do not stir, but cool on buttered plate until just cool enough to handle. Butter hands, pull between hands, back and forth, until too hard to pull. Break into bite size pieces. If desired, add food coloring, or flavor with peppermint.

Yield: 36 pieces
Miss Elizabeth Vickery

TOFFEE

1 stick butter (¼ pound)
1 stick margarine (¼ pound)
1 cup sugar

3 tablespoons water
½ cup chopped nuts
6 ounces chocolate chips

Cook first four ingredients in a large skillet on high heat for 5 to 8 minutes, until brown. Stir constantly.

Place nuts on a cookie sheet and pour hot syrup over them. Cool 2 minutes. Sprinkle chocolate chips over top. When cool break into pieces.

Nancy Voss

Always stir your cake batter in the same direction if you want good luck.

GRAMMA'S TAFFY

1 cup light corn syrup
2 cups white sugar

1 cup whipping cream
Vanilla

Put all ingredients in a large kettle. Place on high heat and cook to boiling. Reduce heat and cook until 255-260 degrees on candy thermometer. Do not stir. Pour out on buttered marble slab to cool. Butter hands first and then use vanilla as necessary when pulling taffy. Pull until light and fluffy and satiny. Put in a buttered pan. Crack into small pieces when cold. 1½ cups of cream has been used and taffy was even better.

Yield: 36 pieces
Robert L. Serviss

MASHED POTATO CANDY

½ teaspoon cream of tartar
1 teaspoon vanilla
1 tablespoon butter
1 cup white potato, mashed

Powdered sugar
2 tablespoons peanut butter
1 teaspoon sugar

Mix cream of tartar, vanilla, butter and potato. Add enough powdered sugar to make a dough. Mix and roll out to ¼ inch thick. Spread peanut butter and sugar on top of dough. Roll as for jelly roll and cut in pieces.

Yield: 2 dozen
Mildred B. Butler

Almost every small community had its cannery to preserve the bountiful summer vegetables and fruits of the area.

PICKLES, JELLIES and PRESERVES

PRESERVED CITRON

3 pounds cut up citron melon
2¼ cups sugar
3 lemons

Pinch of salt (about ⅛ teaspoon)
1 teaspoon vanilla

Peel citron melon and cut in desired shapes. Cover citron with boiling water and let stand for one hour. Drain well. Add sugar and allow sugar to dissolve slowly over very low heat. Stir gently so citron pieces will remain whole. Boil gently, stirring often until citron is clear and syrup is thick. Add juice of 3 lemons, salt, and vanilla. Allow to cool thoroughly as citron will plump. Place a slice of lemon rind in each of four pint jars and fill jars with preserves. Seal and process 10 minutes in boiling water bath so jars will seal.

Yield: 4 pints
Mrs. Ethel Collison

BEACH PLUM JAM

6 cups prepared beach plums
8 cups sugar

1 package powdered pectin

Wash and pit (do not peel) beach plums and measure 6 cups. Add ½ cup water and bring to boil in 8-quart pot. Cook about 3 minutes. Measure sugar and set aside. Add pectin to fruit and just allow to boil. At once stir in sugar. Bring to a full rolling boil that cannot be stirred down. Stir constantly and boil hard one minute. Remove from heat and skim. Ladle into clear hot jars and seal or cover with paraffin.

Note: Beach plums grow on a lovely wild plum tree indigenous to the sandy dunes of the eastern Atlantic Coast from New Brunswick, Canada, to Delaware and Maryland. The fruits resemble large Concord grapes and the flavor is superlative.

Yield: 5 pints
Beth Adams

CHRISTMAS JAM

2½ cups cooked cranberries
2½ cups sliced strawberries
   (fresh or frozen)

1 package powdered pectin
7 cups sugar
1 green lime

Mix cooked cranberries and strawberries. Slice lime into thin slices, then quarter the slices and add to fruit. Bring to boil in a large kettle and add the pectin and then add sugar all at once. Stir constantly and allow to come to a full, rolling boil, that cannot be stirred down. Boil one minute and remove from heat. Skim and pour into jars. Seal or cover with paraffin.

Yield: 4½ pints or 12 jelly glasses
Sara Kidd

NO COOK STRAWBERRY JAM

2 cups of prepared fruit
1 box powdered commercial
   pectin

4 cups sugar

Completely crush, one layer at a time, fully ripe strawberries. Measure into a large bowl. If necessary, add water for exact amount. Thoroughly mix sugar into fruit; let stand 10 minutes. Mix ¾ cup water and pectin in saucepan. Bring to boil and boil 1 minute; stirring constantly. Stir into fruit, continue stirring 3 minutes. A few sugar crystals will remain. Ladle quickly into containers. Cover at once with lids. Set at room temperature (takes up to 24 hours). Store in freezer. If used in 3 weeks, store in refrigerator. Use glass or plastic containers (1 pint or less) with tight fitting lids. Wash, scald and drain, or use automatic dishwasher with hot (150 degrees or higher) rinse water.

Yield: 3 half pints
Margaret Myers

CORN COB JELLY

14 large red corn cobs to make   3 cups sugar
    3 cups juice   1 package pectin

Wash corn cobs well. Cut both ends off to be sure there are no insects in the cobs. Place cobs in large container and cover completely with water. Boil 30 minutes. Remove cobs and strain juice through heavy cloth. Mix 3 cups of the juice with the sugar and pectin. Boil, following directions on pectin package. When thickened to desired consistency, fill jelly glasses and seal with paraffin.

Note: Over 500 jars of this were made and distributed at the 1969 American Farm Bureau Convention. Said to be best when cobs come directly from the field.

Yield: 6 to 8 glasses
Mrs. Roger Easton

CRANBERRY JELLY

1 quart cranberries   1 pint water
1 pound granulated sugar   ½ package powdered pectin

Wash berries and boil in pint of water 10 or 12 minutes or until they mash easily. Put through colander, add sugar, boil (medium heat) 10 or 12 minutes more. Add pectin and pour into 8 molds which have been rinsed with cold water. Set in cool place.

Yield: 8 servings
Mrs. Hubert White

PEACH AND ORANGE MARMALADE

12 peaches   2 oranges

Quarter and seed. Remove white center (leave rind). Grind oranges and peaches together. Measure cup for cup of sugar. Cook 35 minutes from time of starting. (Watch closely, will stick). Put in jars while hot. Seal with wax or lids.

Yield: 5 half pints
Jan Taylor

ROSE GERANIUM JELLY

3 cups water
1 cup washed, stemmed rose
   geranium leaves
6 tablespoons lemon juice

1 package (3½ ounce) powdered
   pectin
4 cups sugar
Red food coloring

Heat water and leaves. Remove from heat. Let stand 15 minutes. Strain and add lemon juice and pectin. Stir until mixture comes to a boil. Add sugar. Bring to rolling boil, boil 1 minute. Remove and skim. Add food coloring. Pour into hot jars. Place small geranium leaf on top and cover with paraffin. Excellent with fruit salad or apple pie.

Yield: 6 glasses
Beth Adams

ZUCCHINI MARMALADE

2 pounds young zucchini squash
Juice of 2 lemons
1 teaspoon grated lemon peel
1 13½-ounce can crushed
   pineapple, drained

1¾ package powdered fruit
   pectin
5 cups sugar
2 tablespoons finely chopped
   crystallized ginger

Peel squash and cut in thin slices. Measure 6 cups squash into a large kettle. Add lemon juice, lemon peel, and crushed pineapple. Bring to boil, lower heat and simmer, uncovered, until squash is tender but holds its shape, about 15 minutes. Add fruit pectin. Place over high heat and bring to a boil. Stir in sugar and ginger. Bring to a full rolling boil and boil hard for 1 minute, stirring constantly. Remove from heat, skim off any foam. Stir 5 minutes to cool slightly and prevent fruit from floating. Ladle into hot sterilized jars, seal with hot paraffin.

Yield: 5 half-pints
Libby Ecker

3 FRUIT MARMALADE

2 oranges
1 large or 2 small lemons
½ grapefruit
5 cups sugar

½ bottle liquid pectin
1½ cups water
⅛ teaspoon soda

Remove skins from fruit, discard any white. Slice very thin. Add water and soda. Bring to boil, cover, simmer 20 minutes. Section or chop fruit. Add pulp and juice to undrained rind. Simmer 10 minutes more. Add 3 cups fruit mixture to 5 cups sugar in large pan. Bring to boil. Boil hard 1 minute, stirring constantly. Remove from heat. Add ½ bottle liquid pectin. Skim off foam with metal spoon. Stir for 7 minutes to cool fruit mixture. Ladle into jars. Cover with paraffin.

Yield: 3-4 pints
Beth Adams

HOT PEPPER JELLY

1½ cups chopped peppers (green
   or red)
1½ cups cider vinegar
6½ cups sugar

25 shakes hot pepper sauce
1 bottle liquid pectin
Green food coloring

Combine first 4 ingredients. Bring to boil. Remove from heat and let stand 20 minutes. Return to heat, boil 2 minutes. Remove from heat, add pectin and coloring. Stir and skim. Pour into hot, sterile jars. Cover with paraffin. Great served with cream cheese as an appetizer or with a fruit salad.

Yield: 8 to 10 glasses
Gladys Whiting

MIXED PICKLE

1 gallon green tomatoes (sliced)
1 dozen onions (sliced)
1 bunch celery (sliced)
½ cup salt
½ dozen green peppers
½ dozen red peppers
1 dozen cucumbers sliced

1 tablespoon celery seed
  (heaping)
1 tablespoon mustard seed
  (heaping)
3 pounds sugar
1 quart vinegar

Mix the green tomatoes, onions and celery together with ½ cup salt and cook 10 minutes. Then add all the other ingredients and cook well. Pack into sterile jars and seal.

Yield: 10 to 12 quarts
Mrs. Manie Lawless

7 DAY SWEET PICKLE

7 pounds medium cucumbers
Water to cover
1 quart vinegar
8 cups sugar

2 tablespoons salt
2 tablespoons pickling spice
  (in cloth bag)

Wash cucumbers and cover with boiling water. Let stand 24 hours and drain. Repeat each day for 4 days, using fresh boiling water each time. On fifth day, cut cucumbers in ¼ inch rings. Combine vinegar, sugar, salt and spices. Bring to a boil and pour over sliced cucumbers. Let stand 24 hours. Drain syrup and bring it to a boil. Pour over cucumbers. Repeat on sixth day. On seventh day, drain off syrup again and bring to a boil. Add cucumber slices and bring to boiling point. Pack into hot jars and seal.

Yield: 6-7 pints
Mrs. John Altfather

PICKLED BEETS
(Colonial Recipe)

12 beets	1 pound honey
1 quart vinegar	2 cups water

Cut off all but 2 inches of beet tops, cook in salt water until tender, peel and slice beets when done. Combine vinegar, honey, and 2 cups water in large saucepan, bring to boil and add beets. Heat to a boil.

Yield: 3 pints
Regina Mueller

MARYLAND SPICED PEACHES

12 pounds whole peaches (cling) if possible	1 quart vinegar
4 pounds sugar	2 teaspoons whole cloves

Make syrup of sugar, vinegar and cloves. Heat to boiling. Drop in peaches and let boil until tender, 10-15 minutes. Put peaches in hot jars. Fill with hot syrup and seal.

Yield: 4-5 quarts
Mary Shawn Horsey

PICKLE RELISH

1 gallon chopped cabbage	2 tablespoons mustard (dry)
1 gallon green tomatoes	½ tablespoon turmeric
1 dozen onions	4 pounds sugar
½ dozen peppers (½ red and ½ green)	1 heaping tablespoon flour
	1 tablespoon celery seed
2 quarts vinegar	2 tablespoons mustard seed

Chop vegetables. Let vegetables stand overnight with 1 cup salt. Drain. Let sugar and vinegar boil. Add vegetables and boil 15 minutes. Mix seasonings and add to vegetables and boil 5 minutes. Put in hot, clean jars and seal.

Yield: 20-24 pints
Kay Everngam

PEACH CHUTNEY

4 cups peeled, pitted, chopped
   peaches (about 3 pounds)
¾ cup cider vinegar
¼ cup lemon juice
1 cup raisins
⅓ cup chopped onion
¼ cup preserved ginger

1 tablespoon salt
1 teaspoon allspice
½ teaspoon cinnamon
½ teaspoon clove
½ teaspoon ginger
7½ cups sugar
1 bottle pectin

Mix all ingredients except pectin. Bring mixture to a boil. Stir and boil hard 1 minute. Remove from heat, add pectin. Skim and stir for 5 minutes. Ladle into jars. Cover with paraffin.

Yield: 12 8-ounce glasses
Nancy Adams

HOT DOG RELISH

5 cups ground cucumber
3 cups ground onions
3 cups chopped celery
2 hot red peppers ground
2 sweet peppers ground
1 quart vinegar

3 cups sugar
2 teaspoons mustard seed
2 tablespoons celery seed
¾ cup salt
1½ quarts water

Combine vegetables, add salt and water, let stand overnight, drain. Heat vinegar, sugar, mustard, and celery seed to boiling. Add vegetables. Bring to boiling. Cook slowly 10 minutes. Seal in hot, sterilized pint jars.

Yield: 5 pints
Regina Mueller

PICKLED WATERMELON RIND

2 pounds watermelon rind
2 cups vinegar
2 cups water
4 cups sugar

1 teaspoon clove
1 stick cinnamon
1 teaspoon whole allspice
1 lemon sliced thin

Pare rind and remove all pink portion. Cut in 2x1x½-inch chunks. Weigh down and soak overnite in a brine of ¼ cup salt, 1 quart water. Drain and rinse, drain. Cook in clear water until tender. Combine remaining ingredients and cook 5 minutes. Add rind and cook until clear. Pack in hot, sterile jars, cover with syrup and seal.

Yield: 4-5 pints
Ruth Adams

SOUR CHERRY JAM

4 cups prepared cherries—about
   3 pounds

7 cups sugar
1 bottle liquid pectin

Stem and pit cherries. Chop fine. Measure 4 cups fruit into large kettle. Add sugar to fruit. Boil hard 1 minute. Stir constantly. Remove from heat, add pectin. Skim and stir 5 minutes. Place in jars, cover with paraffin.

Yield: 3 pints
Beth Adams

PEPPER HASH

12 red peppers
12 green peppers
1 large stalk celery
12 medium size onions
1 medium size head of cabbage

1 quart vinegar
3 to 4 cups sugar
1 ounce white mustard seed
½ ounce celery seed
3 tablespoons salt

Grind vegetables. Cover with boiling water and let stand 5 minutes. Drain. Cover again with boiling water and let stand 10 minutes. Drain. Cover with the vinegar mixture and cook 20 minutes. Seal in hot jars.

Yield: About 10 pints
Mrs. Albert Morris

Herbs for cooking, medicines, and fragrances were often grown right in the flower beds around the homes of pioneer Maryland families.

HERBS
and
MISCELLANEOUS

BOUQUET GARNI (FRESH)

1 sprig thyme
1 sprig parsley
1 small sprig rosemary

1 bay leaf
1 small red pepper pod

Tie together with clean white string or place in cheese-cloth pouch. Boil in soup or stew and remove when cooking is finished. Change and vary the herbs to suit your taste.

Sara Kidd

BASIC POTPOURRI

1 pound dried petals (rose,
    geranium, larkspur, etc.)
30 grams each frankincense,
    myrrh, patchouli, vetiver
    sandalwood chips)
¼ cup gum benzoin
4 to 6 tonka beans

½ vanilla bean
6 cinnamon sticks
¼ cup cinnamon, cloves,
    tarragon, coriander, each
1 to 2 drops rose oil
4 drops violet oil
2 drops jasmine

Grind frankincense, myrrh, tonka beans, and benzoin. Add oils to spices. Add all to petals. Store in covered container at least a month. Package in sachet form or in clear glass, covered containers. Dried rose buds and other small flowers pressed against outside of jars add color and interest.

Beth Adams

LAVENDER POTPOURRI

½ pound lavender flowers
6 drops oil of lavender
1 tablespoon fixative for each
    quart of leaves

2 cups dried red geranium
    blossoms
1 cup each white larkspur and
    white rose petals

Mix, allow to ripen 1 month. Package or enjoy in open bowl. If mixture loses strength, place in covered jar and add a few drops of vodka and fixative from basic potpourri recipe.

Beth Adams

DRIED BOUQUET GARNI PACKETS
(nice for gifts)

¼ cup dried onion flakes
¼ cup dried parsley flakes
¼ cup dried thyme leaves
1 tablespoon each dried
    marjoram, basil, and
    rosemary leaves

4 bay leaves, crushed
2 hot red peppers, crushed with
    seeds
1 tablespoon black pepper corns

Mix all ingredients in a small bowl. Cut a double thickness of cheese-cloth into 4-inch squares. Place 2 to 3 tablespoons of the herb and spice mixture in the center of squares. Gather sides of cheese-cloth together to make a pouch and tie tightly with clean white string. Store in tightly closed container in a cool, dry place. Use in soups, stews, and when boiling or poaching meat, poultry, or fish.

Yield: 12 packets
Sara Kidd

CANDIED VIOLETS

1 egg white
½ teaspoon water

Super fine sugar

Pick violets when freshly opened. Wash gently. Shake dry. Beat 1 egg white slightly. Add ½ teaspoon water. Using small water color brush, brush mixture on both sides of violet. Shake super fine sugar over the blossoms thru a salt shaker. Place on waxed paper, allow to dry, at least 1 day in place free from moisture. Store in covered tin.

    Use to decorate cakes, cookies, petit fours, cupcakes, etc. Entirely edible. Dark violets give best results.

Beth Adams

ROSE JAR

1 quart rose petals
1 cup each lavender and rose
   geranium leaves
½ cup patchouli
¼ cup sandalwood chips and
   vetiver mixed
2 teaspoons frankincense and
   myrrh mixed

1 teaspoon each powdered
   benzoin, cinnamon, cloves
2 tonka beans-ground
¼ cup allspice
10 drops rose oil
1 cup orris root

A basic mixture to which additional petals can be added during the year. Mix, allow to ripen. Place in sachets or glass jars.

Beth Adams

LEMON VERBENA POTPOURRI

1 cup lemon Verbena leaves
1 cup lemon balm leaves
½ cup mixed yellow petals
   (forsythia, marigold, rose,
   calendula, lemon thyme)
Peel of 1 lemon, grated and dried

6 drops lemon Verbena oil
1 tablespoon fixative
   (Frankincense, Myrrh,
   Benzoin or Orris root) for
   each quart of leaves

Combine and allow to stand one month in tightly covered container. Package in sachet form or in clear glass containers.

Beth Adams

GLASS CLEANER

½ cup sudsy ammonia
1 pint Isopropyl Alcohol
1 teaspoon dishwashing
   detergent

Enough water to make one gallon

Use in spray bottle to clean windows, mirrors, etc.

Martha Shipe

MOTH REPELLENT

Use equal parts of peppermint, rosemary, tansy, thyme, and penny royal. Harvest toward the end of summer. Tie in bunches and hang by stems until dry. Rub leaves and blossoms off stems. Sprinkle among clothes and linens. Orange mint, lavender, costmary, southernwood, and santolina may be added.

Jane M. Ewing

"FLO'S" POULTICE
(For colds or "Flu")

1 tablespoon dry mustard
2 tablespoons aqua ammonia
2 tablespoons turpentine

1 tablespoon lard, melted
1 egg

Mix all together and add enough flour to make a medium thick paste. Spread on a thin cloth. Fold cloth like an envelope and place on chest and/or back. Will not blister. May be left on all night. Use 1 teaspoon turpentine for children.

Florence Howard
(from grandmother's cook book)

INDEX

INDEX

I N D E X